R

Return From Krypton

Rational Steps to Entrepreneurial Success

W. Berry Fowler

KRYPTON PRESS

Library of Congress Catalog Number: 96-94518

ISBN 0-9653167-0-X

To my children, Cullen, Nicole, Billy, and Catherine:
May your vision be crystal as you reach to the stars.

Acknowledgments

Throughout my business career there have been many people whose support, encouragement, or simple goodwill have helped me along the way. Some have quite unwittingly contributed to my success through providing the challenges and obstacles that made me stronger and wiser. It is not possible to list all of the people who have helped me in my journey. Still, there are a few key folks whose contributions have been critical. It is with great pride and deeply felt gratitude that I acknowledge them here:

My mother, **Martha Oliver**, who raised me to truly believe, "You can be anything you want to be."

W.C. Berry, who provided countless hours or loving instruction in life's most important lessons.

George Naddaff, the consummate entrepreneur and my early mentor, whose words of encouragement continue to be an inspiration.

Gene Williams, who taught me that wisdom comes from experience.

Dean Wilcox, who shared the game till the end.

Bob Bingham, The Pharaoh of Flexibility, who, through his clear thinking and remarkable communications skills, showed me how excellent business is done.

Acknowledgments

Robin Wes, The Pied Piper of Productive Play, who daily demonstrates his belief that children *are* our future.

Peter Shea, Bob Farrell, and **Robert MacLellan,** who offered encouragement from the start.

Linda Wilcox, who told me, "You really should write a book."

Cindy Sadler, my partner at Krypton International, **Abe Ostrovsky,** and **Stanley Young,** who will help Krypton reach the stars.

Tina-Louise, Paul, Judy, Neil, Chris, Don, Jack, Doug, Dave, and **The Spike Man,** who consistently demonstrate their belief in the Krypton vision.

Mark Schuster and **Tony Riviera** who did me the honor seeking my assistance as they began their entrepreneurial journeys.

Don Mazzella, who said, "You really ought to finish your book."

Lana Sanderson and **Philip Bovenkamp,** a writing team whose talent and enthusiasm for my ideas helped to get the right words on the page.

Walt Disney, whose example has provided inspiration to many young entrepreneurs and whose memory reminds us all to wish upon a star.

And, finally, to **Anne,** my real partner, whose encouragement knows no bounds.

A Note on Gender Usage

Like everyone else, I struggle with the conflict between what is grammatically correct and what is politically correct when it comes to gender usage in language. It's no secret that women are currently opening small businesses at a higher rate than men. It seems odd, then, to defer to the grammatical tradition of using the masculine gender to refer to all entrepreneurs. I've been known to use the word *their* instead of *his* to avoid using gender, but I often end up with a grammatically incorrect sentence that way. So, in this book, I have used both masculine and feminine gender, not necessarily the same number of times. I trust that my readers will be somewhat patient and sensitive to the awkwardness that we all seem to be feeling about this issue. As you read the book, you will discern the level of regard I have for independent thinkers who start their own business. Since more such people are women than men, I hereby go on record with my respect for these business pioneers who have not let gender be an obstacle for them and who, I am confident, will not let gender usages in this book or any other impede their enjoyment or appreciation of the useful information contained.

Contents

CONTENTS

Step Two: Establish Systems For External Operations

Step Three: Establish Systems
For Financial Operations

Avoiding Common Pitfalls

To Krypton
and Beyond

On Thursday, September 3, 1987, I returned from three months on Krypton. It was a magical trip that marked for me the achievement of a dream and yielded a new understanding of business success. I was 38 years old and a multi-millionaire, not what my high school or early college teachers would have predicted for me, I can assure you. Not a bad showing for a kid who had struggled for years with reading deficiencies and had dropped out of college no less than three times. I am eager to tell you about my return from Krypton, but first let me share a little of the history that got me there.

Remember high school? I sure do. It was a great time. I had an active social life, sang in my own rock band, and made the most of life. But academics were a struggle. My grades hovered around and below average, but I got by. I was always quite a talker and showed interest in what my teachers had to say. As long as I didn't have too heavy a reading load, I could do OK in my classes. Most of my teachers thought I was reasonably bright but just not applying myself. I tried to read the assignments, but it was slow-going. My comprehension and retention levels

1

hardly made the struggle worthwhile. What I didn't know and what my teachers didn't recognize was that, like millions of other high school students in our country, I really did not know how to read. Like so many other kids, I had managed to bluff my way through elementary school, junior high, and high school without acquiring a rounded complement of basic reading skills.

When I entered college the game was up. I couldn't fool my way through classes anymore. Three times I started college. Three times I dropped out in frustration. The third time I dropped out of college, I spent six months selling life insurance, an experience I found so harrowing it propelled me back to college for the fourth and final time. Looking back, I sometimes wonder about my tenacity in returning to school. My efforts there had yielded little in the way of academic success, while my "real life," with the exception of the life insurance fiasco, had been fun and lucrative. I started a business when I was nineteen. I opened the first privately owned concession at Marineland in Palos Verdes, California, drawing portraits and caricatures of the tourists. Later, I hired and trained other college students and expanded to a second popular tourist attraction. My small business provided me with a solid income while I attended school. It's a wonder I didn't give up on school when business was so much more fun. Still, I hated losing. The college game was one I was determined to win.

When I enrolled at Chapman College for my fourth shot at a college education, I noticed a poster for a speed reading class. Remembering my many years of frustration being buried in reading assignments, I thought maybe speed reading might be just the thing to handle college academics. I signed up for the course, eager to acquire this new tool. After the second class meeting, the instructor pulled me aside saying, "Berry, I don't want you to take this the wrong way, but speed reading is not what you need." My heart sank. I thought that she was going to tell me it was hopeless, but instead she explained, "After working with you for the past two sessions, I believe you missed out on some very basic information that has created gaps in your reading skills." She went on to explain that by doing some diagnostic testing to identify my strengths and weaknesses she would be able to prescribe a course of action that could yield positive results in a short period of time. I was ready to try anything.

Never underestimate the power of basic reading skills. In just one semester my life changed irrevocably. My grades went from just barely passing to straight A's. But much more important than my grade point average was the way I felt about myself and school. College became a place of tremendous opportunity. It was fun. I liked it. I loved it. Vowing to help others as I had been helped, I became an education major and went on to teach at Sycamore Junior High School in Anaheim, California.

For five years I taught in the public school system. I found I loved kids and loved teaching. As the years passed, however, I began to have concerns about my ability to meet individual student needs within that system. And, I confess, I was becoming increasingly frustrated with the limited financial compensation for doing what seemed to me to be a remarkably challenging and important job.

In December of 1977 I finished up my semester's work and went home to begin my Christmas vacation. I looked around for something to read and saw a little paperback book that my mother had given me for my thirty-first birthday a few weeks before. It profiled the lives of ten people who had become millionaires prior to the age of forty. Reading these profiles and considering the contrast to my own life stirred up some strong feelings. I was a damned good teacher and I worked hard. Still, I was making only a shade over fifteen thousand dollars a year and that included teaching summers. There wasn't much reason to think the situation would get better. Proposition thirteen, a tax cut proposal for the state of California, threatened to increase class enrollment, while reducing the public school budget. Clearly, my economic future was tied more to politics and to longevity than to the quality of my own performance in the classroom. There had to be a better way.

I read the book during the first two days of vacation, returned to work in January and—much to the chagrin and disappointment of many well-meaning relatives and colleagues—I resigned.

"How can you give up the security of your teaching job?" they asked. "Are you out of your mind?"

But I was determined that my financial future would fare better in *my* hands than in the hands of the Anaheim Union High School District.

For several years I had been thinking about how to develop a business opportunity in education. Every day, as a teacher, I would work with students who needed extra help in basic skills. The vast majority were average or above average in intelligence, yet they missed out on some basic skills training early in their education. It was painful for me to see so clearly what these students needed and yet be without the time, tools, and budget to give them the help they deserved. I knew how remarkably my life had changed when I finally received reading skills training at Chapman College. I felt that as many as forty to fifty percent of my students could benefit by similar training. Furthermore, it was evident to me that many parents cared deeply about their children's academic success and were willing to pay for programs to augment the offerings of the public schools. Just as parents might pay for private piano lessons, they would be grateful to find professionals in other areas of study in order to enhance their child's education. I felt I had identified an important, widespread need and a viable market.

Another need involved teachers who, like me, were frustrated with the public school system. These highly-trained professionals were looking for alternatives, not because they didn't like teaching or kids, but because the public school bureaucracy had let them down through ever-increasing enrollment and a diminishing budget. Each day they were being asked to do more policing and less teaching. These fine educators were disheartened by the public's refusal to pass school bond issues at a time when America's children were falling further and further behind students in other countries as measured by standardized tests.

Such thoughts moved me to found Sylvan Learning Centers in February of 1979. The results-oriented curriculum I developed had a remarkable impact. Students were consistently raising their reading level by a full academic year with the first 36 hours of instruction. With that rising reading level came a new-found pride and interest in learning. It was tremendously exciting and gratifying to see these students come alive to learning again.

My first student, Kevin, was a sweet, red-haired, freckle-faced fourth grader with a smile that lit up the room. Kevin came from a close, middle-class family and was pleasant and well-behaved. Because he was quiet and did not pose a behavioral problem for teachers in the public school system, he had largely been overlooked. For overworked teachers, quiet, nice kids often become invisible. Consequently, Kevin's reading problem had not been recognized and he had been passed along from one grade to the next even though his reading skills lagged sorely behind. Finally, by fourth grade, Kevin was desperately frustrated. He would come home from school in tears, convinced that he was stupid and would always be a failure. By the time they came to Sylvan, Kevin's parents were frantic. The most important person in their lives was failing in school. It was not until fourth grade that they realized Kevin had a problem. He just couldn't keep up. The diagnostic tests I administered showed Kevin to be of above-average intelligence and reading at a mid-second-grade level. No wonder his self-esteem was suffering. Every day he was being asked to do work that he couldn't do.

I worked with Kevin through 36 hours of instruction. At the end of that time, I administered the same tests he had taken when he came in. When I sat down to tell Kevin's parents that their son was now reading at a fourth-grade level, there wasn't a dry eye among us. Kevin was the first of many students who would demonstrate that the Sylvan system works and had the potential to positively change young lives.

Wanting to make this help widely available, I franchised Sylvan Learning Centers. There are now almost 600 centers operating worldwide having served over two million students and offering business opportunities to others committed to providing educational assistance to young people.

In 1985 Kindercare, the largest chain of day-care providers in the world, expressed an interest in acquiring Sylvan. With Kindercare's track record in providing quality pre-school education, I knew Sylvan would be in good hands. So on May 10, 1985 I signed the agreement and became a multimillionaire. I was 38 years old.

Intellectually, I knew I had reached one of my major goals by becoming a millionaire before the age of 40. Emotionally, it took a little while to sink in.

Like the stereotypical nouveau-riche guy, I headed straight for the marina and bought a big boat. A *very* big, *very* nice boat. Wanting to give this vessel a powerful-sounding name to reflect my sense of accomplishment, I settled on "Krypton." For nearly three months, my family and I cruised the scenic Pacific waters from Washington state to Alaska. It was a wonderful time of celebration.

It was also a time of reflection. As I stood at the helm of the boat and viewed the beauty around me, realizing that I would never have to work again, I asked myself, "How did this happen?" After all, I'm a pretty ordinary guy. So many people strive to create a successful business and most do not succeed. What did I do right? Had I been smart or lucky, neither or both? Was it just a fluke, or could I do it again? These were my thoughts as I traversed the waters of the Pacific adjusting to the reality of my success.

After five years of semi-retirement—"semi" because I did some consulting for several growth companies, but mostly I played golf, travelled, and had more children—my three-year-old daughter, Nicole, led me to my next business venture. Back in the Seattle area, Nickie enrolled in a gym class. When she would come home after class, she was always exuberant and eager to demonstrate her newly-developed skills. As weeks passed, Nickie displayed growing confidence, poise, and coordination. More importantly, she expressed an increasing enthusiasm for learning, for trying new things, and for bonding with others in her class as the kids offered mutual support and encouragement to one another. Recognizing these skills as a necessary foundation for success in school, I became curious about the program and went to one of her classes to observe. What I had assumed was simply a gym class turned out to be an innovative program that taught children how to listen carefully, follow directions, take appropriate risks, and develop strong bodies and healthy self-images. The whole program, developed by Robin Wes, whom I refer to as the "Pied Piper of Child Development," was set to music, and the kids loved it. I loved it, too. As the old saying goes, I liked it so much, I bought the company. Here I saw an opportunity to do for pre-school children what Sylvan had done for older kids. Applying what I had learned with Sylvan, I franchised the company, naming it "The Little Gym,

International." When I sold my controlling interest in December of 1994, there were nearly 100 franchises operating. Most recently, the count was close to 150 gyms with franchises operating in over a dozen countries.

My success with The Little Gym confirmed my belief that application of proven, replicable techniques greatly enhances the probability of success in operating a business. What I had done involved no magic, no genius, no superhuman powers. What I had done, any competent, determined individual with the right kind of training and support could do.

My ruminations aboard the Krypton had grown into a vision, a vision of providing education and support to the small-business owner and to fledgling entrepreneurs. What follows in this book is the culmination of years of striving and experience—mine and that of many others. You will find practical wisdom here, and my hope is that you will also find just the right kind of encouragement to spark in you the determination and drive to be numbered among the finest, most innovative people I know, the American small-business community.

Pre-Steps

Chapter One

A Call
To Action

Upon the plains of hesitation bleach the bones of countless millions who, on the threshold of victory, sat down to wait, and awaiting, they died.

— Author Unknown

"You have to circulate to percolate," a friend of mine used to say. Jeff was a successful salesman and had quite a repertoire of motivational sayings that he used to keep himself going. I asked him once what that saying meant to him. "Well, nothing good ever comes from just sitting around," he said. "When I get out and start talking to people, that's when I feel my best, that's when I get my best ideas, and that's when I get lucky."

What Jeff found is that breaking through inertia is often the toughest part of any project. Although taking action without a clear sense of direction can result in spinning wheels, ruminating endlessly about direction *without* taking action results in absolutely nothing.

You'll never hear me tell you *not* to do your homework, but beware of over-preparing and under-performing. You've heard the term "anal-retentive" commonly used to refer to someone who is being compulsive or unreasonably concerned about details; one of my friends uses the term "anal-izing" to describe the unproductive nit-picking and what-ifs that occur if discussion and analysis continue beyond the point of productivity. Planning and analyzing can become another way of *not doing it* after a certain point.

A lot of people find the Rocky series of movies, in which Sylvester Stallone plays a prize fighter, quite motivating. In each film there is a moment at which Rocky decides to pursue or defend a title. In some of the films he is, at that point, tired, overweight, or out of shape. Often his friends and family are set against it. But at the moment of decision/commitment, the action begins. You then see Rocky running in the dark on rainy mornings and working out in the gym. His changing view of himself as he begins to visualize success is conveyed in his changing demeanor as he approaches the big fight. He looks and behaves more and more like a winner. Sylvester Stallone may not be the greatest actor who ever lived, but his ability to capture the power of decisiveness and action was the key to the success of the Rocky films. We all identify with Rocky because we understand the importance of committing to a goal, taking action, overcoming obstacles, and preparing mentally and physically for victory.

We all have it in us—a dream, a mission, a calling—whatever you choose to call it. The voice of your better self whispers to you. Sometimes it shouts. One of these days it will say just the right thing at just the right time and you will listen. That moment will change your life.

I sometimes wonder how many great business ideas are generated every day in restaurants and lounges across the country as friends talk and reflect on how things could be different. The number, I'm sure, is staggering. But an idea is just an idea if no action is taken. Without action, the best idea in the world is nothing but fantasy. Occasionally you read about a couple of friends like Todd Holmes and Louis Amoroso, who were complaining about their jobs over a beer one day. They came up with the idea for Beer Across America, a beer-of-the-month club concept. The two had been talking about the success of wine-of-the-month clubs. "Why not beer?" they thought. Why not, indeed? Within three years the two were offered $20 million for their company. They turned the offer down, confident that their business will continue to grow and prosper. When you hear a story like that, does it kind of irritate you? It's because you know full well that you have had equally good ideas, and you just let them go by.

With this book, I hope to challenge you to take action on one of your good, solid ideas and start a business or take your existing business to a new level. It doesn't have to be a unique or completely original idea. After all, a sandwich shop can be a strong, successful business, but it's certainly not original. You don't need a new mousetrap, just a good mousetrap well-packaged and delivered with superior service. This book will help you to envision the nuts and bolts of your own successful business. Equipped with that vision you will be on the verge of success. The next step will be up to you, the step of taking action.

Chapter Two

What's With All These Systems?

If you've glanced through the table of contents of this book, you have already noticed that three out of four of the steps to entrepreneurial success involve establishing systems. "Just what the heck are systems?" you may be asking, "And why do I need them?"

Let's take the first question first. What is a system? In any business transaction there is a sequence of tasks or actions. Once a successful sequence has been worked out, it can then be replicated by yourself or your employees thereby making it unnecessary to perpetually reinvent the wheel. When a set of successful sequences is adopted as your way of doing business, it becomes a system.

Put another way, a system is *an organized, coordinated, and replicable method to achieve a desired outcome*. A system does not have to be a complex and difficult matter. Allow me to offer a simple example. If you purchase pre-printed While-You-Were-Out pads for telephone messages, you will notice they suggest a system. They provide a sequence for recording information. Using them will assure that with each incoming message, the name and number of the caller will be recorded in the same place on the message form. Check-mark boxes allow for a quick indicator as to the action requested (please call, will call back, etc.). If you determine where messages will be placed after they've been recorded, then you've got a system for handling incoming phone messages.

Why does your business need systems? Having systems in place increases efficiency, reduces errors, builds quality control into every aspect of your enterprise, and allows the business to operate properly without your constant supervision. Having systems in place will eliminate the need for repetitious decision-making. Things will be done in accordance to sequences that have been proven to work, to get the results you and your customers expect. These systems will need to be documented. Such documentation will facilitate the training of employees and will build value into your business.

One of the reasons that a good franchise business is considered less risky than an independent start-up is that the systems have already been determined and documented by the franchisor and need only to be put into operation by the franchisee. If you were to purchase a franchise for a hamburger stand, for example, you would also be purchasing systems for every aspect of the business from personnel management to procurement to cooking procedures, all of which would have been developed, field tested, and documented for you. If you start your own independent business, you will benefit from being systems-orientated, doing that same kind of development, testing, and documentation. Not only will your business run more smoothly, but it will have greater appeal to investors.

As I was growing up, my grandfather had a business that involved buying and selling oil refineries that were no longer profitable nor wanted by their current owners. His team would remove all parts and debris from the property. Doing this job safely and in keeping with all environmental regulations was quite a task, and my grandfather was well rewarded for it. After disassembling the refineries, he would sell them to customers. It was not unusual for my grandfather to take down a refinery in Texas and reassemble it in Venezuela. It was a truly international business in its scope, and he was known the world over as one of a relative few who could be counted on to get such a job done right. One year he was even nominated for US Oil Man of the Year. My grandfather had employees who worked for him, but they all worked directly under his supervision. When he decided to retire, his business retired with him. No grandfather, no business. Why? Because he never systematized his business. He never even documented how he did what he did. There were no recruiting and training programs in place, no marketing plans, no customer service guidelines. All of that information was confined to my grandfather's memory. In all those years he really hadn't built a business, he was just self-employed. I don't mean to suggest that there is anything wrong with that. After all, my grandfather certainly made a lot of money during his career. But I would have enjoyed seeing him retire with an even larger nest egg from selling his business. And it could so easily have been done. Establishing systems and keeping records go a long way toward bridging the gap between self-employment and building a viable business. That's why I say that establishing systems builds value and adds equity to your business.

You may not be planning to franchise your business, but it would be useful for you to think of it as if you might. When I started Sylvan Learning Centers, I knew from the beginning that I wanted to make it possible for other teachers in others communities to do what I was doing. So I wrote everything down. I approached every step of the business systematically. How will this work best? How can we do this more efficiently or with less expense? What are peak times for recruiting students and how can we best use our marketing time and energy during off-peak periods? I came up with systems, tried them out, adjusted them to get them to work better, and wrote it all down. By the time Sylvan was franchised, I knew how to teach others to do the business expertly and to be up and running in far less time than it would have taken if they'd had to work all that out themselves. What if I hadn't franchised Sylvan? I would have had documentation to help me train my employees, systems and processes all worked out that would keep the business running smoothly and profitably. I also would have had a highly marketable business for someone who wanted to buy a business of that nature.

Throughout this book we will be referring to systems in different facets of your business. You will be tempted at times to skip the process of developing and documenting a system, but to do so is a false economy. In the long run, systems will save you time over and over again.

Replicable systems. Learn to love the concept. It will make the difference between a frenzied, exhausted proprietor who can't take a week off from his business and one who can leave the business in the hands of his employees knowing that quality will not suffer. It can mean the difference between having a salable business that can yield retirement income for you and a self-produced job that evaporates when you decide to call it quits. In short, it can mean the difference between self-employment and real business ownership.

Step One

Develop Your Vision

Chapter Three

Do You Really Want to be an Entrepreneur?

One of the questions I am frequently asked in interviews is, "Can entrepreneurship be taught?" The underlying assumption seems to be that an entrepreneur is born, not made. It's almost as if some people believe the ability to start and grow a business is genetic. Perhaps that myth has been perpetuated by some of the academic research. Some studies have suggested that having one or more family members who are also entrepreneurs is a positive indicator for entrepreneurial success. This is downright silly. The reason that offspring of entrepreneurs are more likely to be successful entrepreneurs themselves is that they grow up believing that starting a business is a perfectly normal, sane thing to do. They view business success as relatively ordinary and attainable. In much the same way, movie stars' kids often become actors themselves; they see up close and personal that being a movie star is an attainable goal, a viable career option. If you see yourself as the kind of person who can do it, you've won half the battle already. If you see a parent or an aunt or uncle do it, you know that you can, too.

I like to take that projection a little further and say, "If *anyone* can do it, why couldn't *you*?" If you choose a business that truly interests you, arm yourself with the right kind of information, work hard and apply proven business practices, why *wouldn't* you succeed?

"But isn't it risky, Berry?" they ask.

"Compared to what?" I say.

In the fifties when big corporate and government entities offered relatively stable employment, entrepreneurship was thought to be for misfits, for the folks who just couldn't conform to the corporate standard. The nineties have rolled out a very different scenario. Downsizing has displaced literally millions of highly trained, well-educated workers. Many of them, some after numerous relocations and job changes, are now looking to small business ownership for some stability.

When I was in my early twenties, my father had a heart attack. He had been a successful sales manager for a steel company that made industrial shelving and lockers for the grocery and school industries. It took Dad some time to recover his strength and confidence following that event, and during his recovery he couldn't function at his normal 110 percent. Six months after his heart attack, the company president, who had supposedly been his best friend, told him that they couldn't afford to keep him on anymore. My father had given 20 years and every fiber of his being to the company, and yet they let him go. It was then that I realized there was no security in working for someone else. At first I was angry. How could they do that to him? But I soon came to realize that good, bad, or indifferent, that's just the way it was. If I wanted to have control over my own livelihood, I would need to have some kind of business venture of my own. Even during my years of teaching, I ran seasonal businesses in the summer to augment my income.

We all know there are no guarantees in life. There is an element of risk in starting and operating a business, but job security is pretty tough to come by these days, too. So if you're inclined to strike out on your own and you are undeterred by the prospect of long hours, hard work, and heavy responsibility, why not reach for your dream?

There is no denying that starting and growing a business is hard work. After I sold Sylvan, a lot of people told me I was lucky to be able to retire independently wealthy at age 39. Lucky? I just compressed 40 years worth of work into 10 years. That's why I was able to retire young and rich. Nothing lucky about it.

The whole idea of compressing time is something that has always intrigued me. While other people are sitting around thinking about stuff and engaged in what I call "paralysis by analysis," a successful entrepreneur should be off and running. There's a lot to be said for speed in a competitive world. You only have so many years on this planet to do what you want to do. So prepare, do your homework, but then make a decision and get on with it. Kinetic energy is a powerful force. Once you get moving, it's easier to keep moving. Each step you take allows you to see a little further, and the further your vision extends, the more you can hope to accomplish.

When I started Sylvan Learning Centers, a lot of people questioned my credentials for doing so. "Berry," they'd say, "What do you know about reading theory and the huge body of academic research on reading disabilities? What if some of these kids are hyperactive or have learning disabilities (a popular term in the Seventies)? I am amazed at how people often jump at the chance to apply a label to a problem, as if that excuses everyone involved from the responsibility to improve the situation. Frankly, I didn't care why kids couldn't read! The only thing I cared about was figuring out a way to help them read better. The curriculum and teaching techniques I developed at Sylvan worked. They worked so well that we guaranteed them. So, why should it matter what caused the problem, as long as we had the solution? Today, Sylvan Learning Centers continue to help children and adults reach their full potential. Using the same basic curriculum and teaching techniques, Sylvan has helped over two million students.

Still, there were moments when those critics could get to me a little. I recall a time when I was feeling a little uncertain. I did not, after all, hold a Ph.D. or any doctoral level academic degree. I confided in my father, who said to me, "Berry, can you teach kids to read?"

"Yes, I can," I stated.

"And you developed the Sylvan technique for teaching kids to read?"

"Yes, I did."

"Then you have nothing to feel uncertain about. You are the ultimate expert in your own business, the ultimate expert in the Sylvan teaching methodology."

I'll never forget those words. And I offer them as advice to you. There will always be people with more credentials or more experience than you. But once you own your own business, you will be the ultimate expert in that business. It belongs to you and you have the right and the responsibility to lead and direct the development of that business.

It might interest you to know that in 1985, former Secretary of Education, Terrel H. Bell, became a member of Sylvan's advisory board. For me, that settled the question of credentials. For you, it should illustrate the importance of forging ahead with what you know will work. It's not always the super-experts that come up with the best solutions to problems. I was a junior high school classroom teacher when I developed the methods that were later endorsed by a former Secretary of Education. There's a lot to be said for thinking big while you're in the trenches. Trust what you know.

K K K K

Now I'd like to introduce you to Duncan, a friend of mine. Duncan's a hypothetical entrepreneur who, with his sister, Denise, has been running a part-time business from his home for nearly a year. They have enjoyed a certain measure of success, and they're encouraged about the future of the business. Now they're ready to take things to the next level. For Duncan and Denise's business, this means leasing a building, hiring a couple of employees, and doing a lot of other things most businesses do. Just as important, it means Duncan will quit his job as an x-ray technician at St. James' hospital. We're going to follow Duncan and Denise through this process. At the end of each chapter, we'll revisit them, and I'll use their struggles and successes to illustrate the principles covered in the chapter.

But first, let me take you back to when Duncan started to feel his first real entrepreneurial urges about 12 months ago. Duncan was unhappy working at St. James'. He was facing many of the same frustrations that I faced years ago when I taught public school. One reason Duncan had chosen a career in the health care industry was that he wanted to help comfort the sick and the injured, but with all the budget cuts and under-staffing and the volume of people who needed x-rays everyday, Duncan felt like he was doing anything but comforting people. X-raying children was particularly disheartening. He had to force injured children to remain still while he x-rayed them, and he just didn't have time to calm and reassure his young patients the way he wanted. Besides all this, he was underpaid and unappreciated, and a friend of his had just lost a similar job at a local clinic leaving Duncan a little uncertain about his own job security.

Duncan had recently come up with an idea to help with x-raying children. With Denise's help, he designed and made a pillow shaped like a friendly panda bear with all four legs spread like it was ready to hug someone. The pillow was firm yet flexible enough so that its legs could be wrapped around a child and fastened in the back. Duncan's original purpose for the pillow was to assist him in keeping a child still during an x-ray, but he discovered an additional benefit. Many children were calmed when hugged by the soft bear. Here's what it looked like:

It wasn't long before Jonesy, another x-ray technician, asked Duncan to get him his own "animal."

"Animal?" Duncan asked.

"You know," Jonesy said. "Like your pillow-animal, your Pilanimal. I'd pay you for it."

That's when Duncan first got the idea to start his own business. The more he thought about it, the more the idea appealed to him. By going into business for himself, he could escape the frustrations of working at the hospital, he could take control of his future, and he could still help to comfort those who were sick or injured.

But what did he know about running a business? Could he really afford to take the risk? He wasn't just gambling with his own life. He was a divorced dad with custody of a ten year old son. Wouldn't it be irresponsible to put Bret's future on the line for some crazy scheme? But no, America was full of people just like him who had struck out on their own and made their lives better. If they could do it, then why couldn't he?

So Denise started sewing Pilanimals and Duncan took them with him to work. It wasn't long before they'd saturated the market at St. James', and Duncan began stopping by the other two hospitals and the clinics in town. Soon he was traveling to nearby towns on his days off to sell Pilanimals. Sometimes a hospital would buy several; sometimes individual technicians would buy a couple; but Duncan rarely made a stop without selling at least one.

It was a great idea, but nobody was getting rich from it. They sold Pilanimals for $20 apiece, most of which was profit. On a good day, Duncan might make a couple of hundred dollars and split it with Denise. He began to wonder if it was really worth the hassle, but he knew Pilanimals were a good idea. He had proven it to himself, and he wasn't willing to let it go.

It had become clear to Duncan and Denise that they would have to expand their business if it was going to survive. Duncan had called on every hospital within driving distance, and, while they'd gotten some repeat business, there had not been enough to keep them going. Duncan had some ideas for increasing sales, but he wouldn't have been able to implement them if he continued to work another job, so he and Denise made up their minds to go into the Pilanimal business full-time.

All the doubts that Duncan had when they first started making Pilanimals came back. Only this time, there was no safety net. If he quit his job and things didn't work out, what would he and Bret do? What made him think he could run a business? What right did he have to sacrifice Bret's security for a pipe dream?

It was Denise who had assuaged Duncan's apprehension the first time, and she came through for him again. "Have you ever really looked at the people who own every other small business in town?" She asked. "They don't have anything on us. If they can do it, then so can we."

"And besides," she added, "You are the ultimate expert in the Pilanimal business."

Chapter Four

Excuse Me, Do You Have the Time?

When my son, Cullen, was in his early teens he began to have some minor problems resulting from the powerful pull of peer influence. I realized that peer pressure was a normal occurrence for kids at that age, but he was experiencing a conflict between his better judgment and his feelings of loyalty to friends who were dabbling in risky behavior. I felt a little intervention was in order. I knew that Cullen would need to make his own decisions about the value of his peer group and their activities, but I wanted to urge him to keep things in perspective. I asked my son how long he expected to live. The question startled him, but he seemed willing to play along.

"I don't know, Dad. Until about eighty, I guess."

"OK, let's draw a horizontal line with zero at the beginning and eighty at the end. The halfway mark would be forty. The quarter mark is twenty. Let's mark where you are at age sixteen."

Cullen watched with detached interest as I constructed the graphic.

"You know, Cullen, up until now you have lived a good life, learned a lot, and built skills that will serve you well for a lifetime. You've made some mistakes, perhaps, but nothing that will irrevocably mar your future. By your own estimate, you have more than three quarters of your lifetime left to live. When did you meet the people you are currently friends with?"

Cullen indicated that he'd been close with his current friends for about a year. We marked it on the timeline.

"All I'm asking, Son, is that you think about it. It's your life. You have to decide how important these friendships are in the whole scheme of things. But when you're considering where your loyalties lie, just don't forget the responsibility you have to yourself, the responsibility to respect and guard the quality of all this." I pointed to the timeline.

You never know, as a parent, if the talks you have with your kids will be meaningful to them. All you can do is try and hope. But that little graphic exercise had an impact. Cullen *did* think about it and made some good choices about his social alliances.

As you go through the process of evaluating what you want in life and from your business, I would like to suggest a simple but powerful exercise. Like the timeline I did for Cullen, this exercise will yield a visual representation that will make the abstract a little more concrete. Everyone I know who has taken the time to do this has found it to be a powerful tool. So, please, don't just glance at this chapter in the book! Take the handful of minutes required to fill this out and consider its implications.

1. Draw a grid like the one on page 31.
2. On line A write your name.
3. On the other lettered lines, write the names of people in your life who are important to you. These might include a spouse, parents, children, siblings, friends. Extend the grid as far as necessary.

4. Above column one fill in the current year.
5. Above column two fill in the year five years from today.
6. Above column three fill in the year ten years from today.
7. Above column four fill in the year fifteen years from today.
8. Above column five fill in the year twenty years from today.
9. Now use the grid to fill in your age this year, five years from now, ten years from now, etc.
10. Do the same with the ages of each of the people on the lettered lines.

	1	2	3	4	5
A					
B					
C					
D					
E					

Many people find this exercise quite sobering at first. It's not necessarily fun to be reminded that you do not have forever to do the things you want to do. But after the initial impact, there can be a real sense of empowerment in this exercise. You begin to have a renewed sense of urgency about what is most important to you. You may see, for example, that if you've been wanting to add a family room onto your house for the kids, that you'd better do it soon, or they will be off to college. You may have always dreamed of taking your parents on a cruise. The timeline will remind you to get that plan into action while your parents are in good health and can enjoy it. While you're looking at it, also note when you might like to retire or make other major lifestyle changes. This will help you in the planning of your business. You will want your business to yield the income, the independence, the flexibility to accommodate your dreams for yourself and for your loved ones.

𝕂 𝕂 𝕂 𝕂

When Duncan was first considering quitting his job to go into the Pilanimal business full-time, he performed the timeline exercise. It turned out to be one of the things that helped him make his decision. Here is what Duncan's timeline looked like:

	1997	2002	2007	2012	2017
Duncan	36	41	46	51	56
Bret	11	16	21	26	31
Denise	38	43	48	53	58
Mom	59	64	69	74	79
Grandpa	81	86	91	96	101

The first thing that struck Duncan when he completed this exercise was the time he had left with Grandpa, his mom's father. Grandpa was healthy for an octogenarian, and he probably had several years left, but not so many that Duncan could afford to waste any. Grandpa had always supported Duncan, had always been there for Duncan's big moments. He had rarely missed any of Duncan's basketball games from his first little league game back in second grade to the game where he twisted his knee and ended his college basketball career. Grandpa was at the hospital with Duncan, too, when they x-rayed the knee and Duncan first considered becoming an x-ray technician. He was at the hospital again when Duncan's son was born. In fact, Bret was named after Grandpa. And now, if Duncan was going to start a business, and especially if it was going to be a success, he wanted Grandpa to see it happen.

Some of the other numbers on the timeline caught Duncan's attention, as well. Bret would probably leave for college in less than ten years. Duncan and Denise both had about 20 years before they'd like to retire. If they were going to do something like this, now was the time. And Mom. Mom had been retired for nearly four years after working for the postal service ever since Dad had died 20 years before. Although Mom got by on her pension, Duncan wanted to be able to help her enjoy her retirement a little more while she was still in good health. But it was Duncan's desire that Grandpa see him succeed that really motivated him, and that was fitting. It had always been Grandpa who had motivated Duncan.

You *Can* Get There From Here: Developing a Vision

Every achievement begins with a vision. It may be a sophisticated, highly-developed vision, or it may be little more than a vague idea.

Cognitive psychologists believe that visualizing change greatly enhances one's ability to make that change. One of the early pioneers in this kind of thinking was Maxwell Maltz, author of *Psychocybernetics*. Dr. Maltz was a plastic surgeon. Although in most cases, a surgical correction of an abnormality would lead to increased confidence in his patients, he noticed that some of his patients continued to behave as if the defect were still there. Some, despite remarkable improvement in their appearance, would insist that they looked the same and would continue to behave as if they were unattractive. This led Dr. Maltz to theorize that internal self-image was more powerful than concrete reality. If this were the case, how might we access and change our self-image and thereby change our lives for the better? His studies led him to believe that the process of visualizing a positive outcome could focus the conscious and subconscious abilities of the mind and greatly enhance one's odds of success.

More contemporary motivational gurus, like Wayne Dyer, echo this finding in slogans such as "You'll see it when you believe it." Sports psychologists use mental practice and visualization to help their clients perform better and win more consistently.

Visualization is, of course, nothing new. In the form of prayer, meditation, hope, and daydreams, it has always been practiced. Negative visualization is even more common; we call it worry! Why not use that energy to help rather than hinder? Visualize victory, strength, and success!

Can you picture an ideal day in your life? Can you picture it replete with sensory detail? I believe it is important to be able to see, in the mind's eye, where we're going, where we want to end up.

Perhaps the single most remarkable example of visualization is the moon-landing. President Kennedy commissioned NASA to put a man on the moon at a time when technology was not sufficiently developed to support such a project. NASA didn't just pump up the space program and wait to see how it went. They started with the goal in mind and worked backward. What will we need to get there, they asked? In this way, their interim goals became clear to them and, ultimately, the final goal was reached.

Knowing where you want to end up is, I believe, critical for you. Yours may be the only hand at the helm. It will be your vision that will inspire others in your organization to give their best. It will be your confidence in your vision that will move others to respect and trust in your business goals.

It has been said that the human mind is teleological in nature. Like a heat-seeking missile, or a flower bending toward the sun, your mind will pick up the subtlest of cues once it has been programmed with a goal. If you know what you want, your senses, both overt and subtle, will seek out your targets and alert you to course corrections needed along the way to ensure goal completion and success.

My own way of creating a vision is pretty straightforward. I believe in sitting down with pen and paper and writing out a description of the perfect day as you would like it to be five years in the future, or ten, or whatever time frame you choose. Because sensory detail is important to give your vision persuasive power in your own mind, you should think hard about the little details. Where will you be living and with whom? What kind of clothes will you be wearing? Will you be going to work? If so, where, by what mode of transportation? Picture your home. Picture yourself in it. See yourself in your kitchen. Walk to the window and look out. What do you see? You get the picture. Details are important. Ask yourself many little questions as you think it through. I believe it is important to do this exercise once for your personal life and, in another sitting, once for your business life. Then check the two visions for compatibility. Will your business, as you envision it, support the lifestyle you envision? Will it give you the flexibility and freedom to live as you choose?

Revisit these descriptions regularly. Each time you will come up with more information. And remember, the power is in the sensory detail. How does it look, smell, taste, feel? Look for pictures in magazines, or symbols of your perfect life—anything that adds concreteness to the vision.

As you may have gathered already, I'm not exactly a touchy-feely kind of guy. I am interested in results. I'm not recommending you use your time to daydream just for fun. I have seen that developing a vision of the future is a way to achieve greater success. Those who decide to start a business and then just wait to see how things go, tend not to go very far. Write down what you're going to do, then make it real.

Some cognitive psychologists recommend inducing a state of deep relaxation before picturing the ideal future. They believe this imprints more effectively on the subconscious mind and brings more of your mental capabilities to bear on making the vision a reality. Can't hurt. Sometimes while working on my vision during a deep relaxation state I have had little surprises pop up, things that I may not have thought of in a normal waking state. So maybe there is something to this business of accessing the subconscious mind.

One way or another, you need to know where you want to go. And you need to believe in your ability to get there.

К   К   К   К

After doing the timeline exercise in the last chapter, Duncan sat down with a notebook and a pencil and started writing a description of a perfect day five years from now. When he awoke on a Monday morning, he could hear Bret getting ready for school downstairs. Bret had to be at school early for basketball turnout—they were running two-a-days—so Duncan got up and offered Bret a ride to school. When he returned, Duncan sat at his kitchen table and enjoyed a cup of coffee, and Grandpa came down from his room.

Apparently Grandpa was living with them in the perfect future. This was something that Duncan hadn't realized he wanted. He'd always known how important being near his grandpa was, but the thought of Grandpa living with him had never occurred to him.

Duncan continued the vision exercise. As he did he discovered other things that were important and also realized that a few things he'd thought were pretty important really didn't matter to him much.

Chapter Six

Prepare to Defend Your Vision

You always hurt the one you love. Or so the old song goes. If you're lucky, your loved ones will support you wholeheartedly in your aspirations. But if they don't, you're not alone. And, if they don't, it's probably not because they don't love you, but precisely because they do. Loved ones don't want to see you get hurt. They don't want to see you take risks. Think back on your childhood when you were learning to ride a bike. In your mind, all you could see was a picture of mastery, a vision of yourself joyously riding your bike with the control and competency of your older, more-experienced friends. All your poor mom could see were scrapes and bruises, tears and close-calls. Now that you're grown and wanting to start a business, don't expect your mom to react much differently than she did with the bike. In a like manner, your friends, your spouse, your siblings may be reluctant to give you wholehearted encouragement to take such a big step. They may just want to protect you, but the image that comes to mind is that of an old ceiling-sprinkler fire protection system. You plan a special meal. You set a beautiful table complete with flowers, beautiful dishes and linens, and lovely candles. You serve the sumptuous meal and light the candles. Sensing the little bit of heat and smoke from the candles, the sprinkler system goes off. It only wants to protect you. There *was* fire, after all. Sometimes we could do with a little less protection.

It's also true that those who have a vested interest in your life may not want you to change. If you change, the way you relate to them might change. They may feel alienated, or threatened, or left out, or left behind. They may even be jealous. And going into business for yourself certainly has the potential to change you.

I remember an evening just before I opened the doors of my first Sylvan Learning Center in Portland, Oregon. I felt it was important to meet with as many teachers as possible to explain Sylvan's unique services and to develop a basis for referrals. With this in mind, I had arranged for my wife and I to meet a couple for dinner. They were teachers who had expressed an interest in learning about the resources that Sylvan would offer. We met at one of my favorite restaurants in the old section of town. My spirits were high as I explained what Sylvan was all about and how I planned to work with students that the public schools were not well-equipped to help. Their enthusiastic response to the Sylvan concept was encouraging. Because they expressed such an interest, I shared my vision of what I knew Sylvan could do for kids.

"I'm going to make this work, and I'm going to franchise the system so that other teachers can have this opportunity and millions of kids can benefit from better reading skills and enhanced self-esteem," I told them. "Before long there will be Sylvan Learning Centers in every major city in the country."

By the end of the evening, I was feeling great about Sylvan, about its value to students and teachers alike, and about the future in general. But my wife seemed sullen and withdrawn. On the drive home, she was silent. Finally, I asked her, "Honey, what's wrong?"

"You really embarrassed me tonight," she said. "You shouldn't be telling people that Sylvan will be a national company. You're just getting started. You can't possibly know how things are going to go. When you talk about all your big plans, people think you're crazy!"

I'll never forget the feeling I had at that moment. It was hard enough to accept the fact that she didn't believe in me, but to think that my enthusiasm, my vision, was an embarrassment to her! Although, on some level, I could understand her feelings, it was essential for me to believe wholeheartedly in my dream. I saw it so clearly, I couldn't *not* believe it! And I couldn't restrain myself in order to stay in *her* comfort zone.

It's an unfortunate fact that not all of your relationships will survive the changes in your life brought about by starting a business. I am no longer married to the woman whom I embarrassed that evening. As my business progressed, she and I had less and less to share. And before long, we both knew it was time to go our separate ways.

Over the years I have stayed in touch with Gary and Dee, the couple we dined with that night. They've become cherished friends. I once asked them if they remembered our conversation of that evening.

"Yes," they said, "We've discussed it many times and have been proud to tell our friends how we dined with the founder of Sylvan Learning Centers and heard him articulate the future of Sylvan, a future that has grown to reality."

In the early stages of preparing your vision, doing your research, and starting your company, you may find yourself vulnerable to the doubts of others. It's perfectly natural to have some doubts of your own. Then, when others question your good sense, it can compound and possibly deter you from proceeding. This phenomenon is so common that in some circles, the term "dream stealers" is used to describe friends and family that serve as doubting Thomases.

Suffice it to say, you need to be a little careful about who you talk to, or—more importantly—who you listen to! The best thing I did for myself during that period of time was to focus on what I called "Individuals of Inspiration." I identified people who, through their words or examples, inspired me to move forward. Some of these individuals were people I knew and trusted and could actually go talk to. Some were people I knew of through reading. I read at length about Walt Disney, Ray Krok, Fred Smith, and Dave Thomas. Whenever my courage began to falter, I would turn to one of these examples and tell myself, "I can do this."

Another technique that I developed then, and continue to use to this day, is something I call the Motivational Drawer. I have a drawer in my desk where I keep symbols of success. I have a photograph of my wife and our four children, a brochure from an exclusive cruise ship that sails to the most exotic ports, a model of a Gulfstream Starship, an up-to-date brochure from Mercedes Benz, the latest copy of *The Rob Report*, and a large check I've made out to myself and dated for my fiftieth birthday.

K   K   K   K

Most of Duncan's co-workers thought he was crazy to quit his job. His boss asked him to stay but, when Duncan declined, told him not to come back when he "fell on his face;" his job would already be taken. And his friends at Bartles' Pub never did take his new business seriously. But there were two people who, more than any of the others, seemed determined to convince Duncan to forget the whole idea: his mom and his ex-wife, Lorraine.

Duncan's mom discouraged him out of love; Lorraine was more spiteful. Mom didn't want to see him fail. Lorraine seemed afraid he might succeed. Mom was scared for Bret's sake. Lorraine used their son as a pawn against Duncan. And while Lorraine was just a nuisance, Duncan's mom got him really discouraged for awhile.

But Grandpa did what Grandpa had always done for Duncan. He talked him through the tough times and gave him the encouragement he needed. Duncan soon learned that there were certain times, times he was particularly susceptible to discouragement, that he just couldn't be around his mom. During those times he had to go see Grandpa.

Duncan also used the motivational drawer technique to stay excited about his goals. In it he kept three items. The first was a set of Mickey Mouse ears. When Duncan was 12, a few years before his dad had died, Duncan, Denise, Mom, Dad, and Grandpa had all gone to Disneyland together. Now Duncan wanted to do that for Bret. And he hoped to do it while Grandpa could still go along, too. The second item was a set of mock basketball tickets. He and Grandpa managed to take in two or three Pistons games each year, but Duncan wanted season tickets, and he wanted really good seats. And the last item was just for Duncan. It was a model of a '65 Ford Mustang, like the one Duncan had when he was in high school except that this one was a convertible.

Whenever Duncan got discouraged, he opened the drawer. One of these things usually motivated him.

Chapter Seven

What's This Business All About?

To promote the healthy and successful physical and mental development of the children of the world, and thereby help our franchisees achieve their business and personal goals.
—Mission Statement of The Little Gym International

Over the last decade it has become something of a corporate fad to have a mission statement. A survey done in 1994 indicated that nine out of ten of the Fortune 500 companies had mission statements or had used a mission statement in the previous five years. Sometimes fads are silly, but sometimes things catch on because they truly are valuable. I believe the mission statement, if properly formulated and well-used, can serve a number of important purposes in an organization.

First, a mission statement can answer the question posed by the title of this chapter, "What's this business all about?" In other words, it can announce to the world what you want to accomplish with your business. It should articulate the central goals and direction of your company in a way that is meaningful to you and understandable to others.

Second, the mission statement can unify and motivate employees of the company by emphasizing the common goals of the organization beyond that of making a profit. We all need a sense that we are working for something more than money; we need a sense of purpose. A well-articulated and sincere mission statement can provide that common sense of purpose.

Third, the mission statement should help members of the organization keep an eye on the bigger picture. In the many hassles and stresses of everyday operations, it is surprisingly easy to lose sight of longer-range goals. The mission statement can serve as a transcendent vehicle, making the larger goals of the organization more accessible and, therefore, more easily applicable to daily interactions and decisions.

A powerful mission statement can:

- K Help to forge an identity for the company in the minds of its people, its customers, and its community
- K Simplify decision making by providing a measure against which decisions are held
- K Reflect the values of your organization, thereby inspiring you and your people by being worthy of your best performance
- K Play a role in recruiting and staff selection by appealing to candidates with compatible values who are likely to be more enthusiastic about working for your company and more likely to contribute wholeheartedly to the fulfillment of your mission

Once you are ready to start writing, keep the following guidelines in mind:

K Be clear and concise
K Use direct language that is clear and memorable
K Capture your operating philosophy and goals
K Define what your company does

Once you've determined your mission statement, use it. You will be proud of it, and you should be. Have it painted on a wall in your reception area or printed on wallet cards or on a poster. Put it where you and others can see it. Use it in brochures, in performance reviews, and at meetings. Revisit it often to keep it alive. One of my colleagues sums up the ingredients of a mission statement as "People, passion, and purpose." Your mission statement will reflect the values of yourself and your people; it will spark your passion, and remind you of your purpose. Used well, your mission statement will save you lots of wheel-spinning and move you surely toward your goals.

K   K   K   K

As Duncan and Denise prepared to expand their Pilanimal business, Duncan suggested that they develop a mission statement to help them form an identity and stay focused on their purpose. "What exactly is our purpose as you see it?" Denise asked.

"I suppose we're both here to make some money," Duncan said. "But for me it's more than that. This business gives me a chance to realize some of the goals I had in going to work for the hospital but that the bureaucracy there had stifled."

"And those are?"

"When I blew out my knee back in college, I had to get it x-rayed. At the hospital I saw kids, little kids, hurting and scared to death. I decided then that I wanted to do something about it.

Becoming an x-ray technician didn't give me the chance I'd hoped for, but now, with these Pilanimals, I really think that I can accomplish what I couldn't before. I won't get the one-on-one contact, but hopefully I'll be able to reach a lot more kids."

"I think that's pretty compatible with how I see our business," Denise said. "When I worked at the department store doing alterations, I learned to really hate sewing. But there's something about knowing that the finished product is going to help calm a hurting child that makes it quite fulfilling."

They began to brainstorm mission statement ideas. "How about something simple like 'To help hurting children'?" Duncan suggested.

"I like it, but it's too general," Denise said. "If we're going to use it to help us stay focused and make decisions, we're going to need a mission statement that's a little more defined. How about 'To produce products that calm and comfort pediatric patients and assist the x-ray process'?"

"Some of the language is good, but it might be too specific," Duncan said. "I can see us developing other products that aren't necessarily used during x-raying and that might not be used only for children."

After discussing ideas and playing with the language, Duncan and Denise agreed on a statement both felt reflected the mission of their business perfectly: *To produce products that calm and comfort anxious patients and thereby facilitate treatment.*

Establish Systems For Internal Operations

Chapter Eight

Site Selection:
What's a Nice Business Like Yours Doing in a Place Like This?

There's an old line that goes, ask any real estate agent what the three most important factors in considering a property are, and he'll respond, "Location, location, and location." He's right, of course, but there are finer considerations that you'll need to take into account to determine what makes a location right for you. There are a couple of other factors (lease costs, facility considerations), which aren't solely matters of location, that you'll also need to consider when selecting a property. Here is a list of things to keep in mind when making this decision:

- **K** Accessibility
- **K** Visibility
- **K** Lease Costs
- **K** Resource availability
- **K** Competition
- **K** Zoning ordinances
- **K** Facility considerations
- **K** Safety

Accessibility is the most important element of location for most companies, but the reasons why it is so important vary from business to business. The kind of location that will be suitable for your company will also vary depending on your type of business. For a business that relies on walk-in customers, such as clothing stores or hair salons, the primary concern with location is proximity to target customers. These kinds of businesses need to be visible and accessible. They need to be near where people live, work, and play. Often this means being near other stores. It doesn't matter whether most of their customers come in on a whim when passing by or schedule appointments and make special trips; if a business doesn't have convenient access, people will find another one that does.

Other businesses use their offices only as a base. They might send employees out to perform services such as cleaning homes, caring for lawns, or spraying for insects. Or they might send sales representatives out to call on homes or other businesses. This kind of business also needs to be located near target customers, but for a different reason. Their locations don't necessarily need to be accessible to their customers, but they need to be able to efficiently access their clients. A service company that has difficulty getting to its customers risks providing poor service and will likely incur unnecessary costs. Likewise, a sales company won't want its sales representatives accumulating unnecessary travel expenses or spending time on the road that could better be spent selling the company's products.

A manufacturing company must also consider the accessibility of a potential site, but more as it pertains to their proximity to material suppliers than to customers. A manufacturer will want to ensure that necessary supplies are easily and quickly available to the location at an affordable price. The wrong location may force a manufacturer to use a more expensive vendor or pay higher shipping costs. It could also mean delays in receiving shipments if the location is too far from the nearest supplier or isn't on a regular freight route.

This is not to say that manufacturers shouldn't consider their target customers when choosing a location. Ideally, a manufacturer will be close to both its material supply and its market. But when it's one or the other, the material supply wins out more often than not. A manufacturer's raw materials quite often come from just a few sources in large quantities while the finished product is shipped in smaller units to many destinations. This is why oil refineries, for example, are in Texas near the raw material rather than in California where there is a large market for the finished product.

When it comes to analyzing lease costs, there are two questions you will need to ask. 1) Is this a fair rent for the property? 2) Can my business afford it? Your real estate agent will be able to give you some idea whether the properties you're considering are priced competitively, but the only way you're going to know for certain is to look at enough different properties to provide you with a good cross section of what is available. Looking at several properties, of course, is a good idea anyway. When considering whether your business can afford a particular property, you should refer to your projections. Later, when we cover financial operations, I'll teach you to develop sales and expense projections that will enable you to determine the financial viability of your business. One of the expenses you'll project is rent. Is the rent the property owner is asking in line with what you budgeted? If it's not, you may have underestimated your rental costs. If this is the case, you should recalculate your projections using the new rent figure. This is the only way you can determine whether your business can be profitable with additional rental expense.

Resource availability is important to every business, not just manufacturers. Resources include raw materials, utilities, and human resources. I'm currently working out of Spokane, Washington. I've noticed several large corporations moving into this area recently, and it's not difficult to figure out why. The city is large enough that resources are available. Spokane is the largest city between Seattle and Minneapolis, which means that a lot of shipping goes through Spokane. There is a large enough work pool here to support large corporations, but salaries are considerably lower than what a company would have to pay in Southern California or even Seattle. And utilities are less expensive here than in most parts of the country. Available resources at affordable rates: Why wouldn't corporations consider locating in Spokane? Chances are you'll be looking to stay a little closer to home than larger companies might be, but you'll want to consider these same resource availability factors when evaluating locations.

Competition can be an important factor in the site selection process. You generally won't want to open a retail store right next door to an established store selling the same products or offering the same services as you. There may be situations, though, when this is not just acceptable but preferable. A clothing store might consider it an advantage to be in a mall with many other clothing stores. The questions to ask are, "Is there enough business to go around?" and "Can I compete in this environment?" You should refer to the market analysis you'll do for your business plan to help you answer these questions.

Before you lease a facility, you should always check with the local municipality to find out what the zoning regulations are, what licenses and permits are necessary, and if there are any other local laws or ordinances that may affect your business. There's a small, conservative town in the northwest corner of Washington state, for instance, that has an ordinance that prohibits serving alcohol in a dancing establishment. That's fine; they like their quiet, little town the way it is, but you wouldn't want to find out about this rule on the night you opened a nightclub there.

There are other factors to consider when deciding what property to lease that have little to do with location. You need to make sure the facility itself meets your needs. Here are a few of the questions you'll want to ask yourself:

- **K** Is the building large enough to meet your needs?
- **K** Does it provide you room to grow?
- **K** Is it laid out in a way that suits your needs?
- **K** Does the property have features you'll need? (loading bay, warehouse)
- **K** What modifications will you need to make? (don't overlook handicapped access and rest room requirements if they apply to your business)
- **K** What repairs will be necessary? (plumbing, electrical, general property improvements)
- **K** Is parking sufficient for your needs?
- **K** Are there safety considerations?
- **K** Is the appearance of the property consistent with the image you want to portray?

We've approached site selection with the assumption that you will be leasing property. This isn't necessarily the case. While most new, small businesses will not have enough capital to be able to purchase property, it may be something you will want to consider. The next chapter offers advice on leasing.

For some businesses, you may not need to find a new site at all. Many service businesses can be run from home, and many small, manufacturing businesses can be set up in a garage or shop. Before you make that decision, though, you'll want to apply the same criteria you'd apply to any other potential site.

Selecting the right site for your business is important. Take your time and consider all the factors that separate a good location from a bad one. Consider accessibility by customers and to suppliers. Think about lease or purchase costs, resource availability, competition, zoning ordinances, and facility considerations. You don't want to rush out and lease the wrong property. After all, you're going to be spending a lot of time there.

K K K K

Duncan and Denise contacted a real estate agent and asked her to show them some properties. They didn't need a lot of room, they explained, just enough for a couple of offices, a production room that could hold six or eight sewing stations and a couple of tables, and some storage space. They looked at four sites one morning, none of them quite right. It was worthwhile to see what was available, though, and to find out what the different places rented for.

The first place they looked at after lunch showed some promise for $750 a month. It was a 900 square foot unit in a light industrial complex with a rest room in the back corner. There were glass doors in the front and an overhead door in the back where there was truck access. The unit on one side was used as an office and warehouse for a construction company. On the other side was the office of a mail-order marketing company. Both Duncan and Denise liked it, so when they got home they asked themselves the questions I suggested earlier in this chapter:

Is the building large enough to meet your needs?

It was small, that's for sure. Fifteen by sixty feet is about the size of a lot of mobile homes. But they got out some graph paper and drew it to scale. In the front, they mapped out a reception area that would also function as an office for the bookkeeper, 10' x 15'; behind that they sketched an office for Duncan and Denise, 10' x 11'; they put a hall leading past the office to the work area, 4' x 10'; and that left a 15' x 40' area (less the rest room) for work and storage, enough room for several sewing stations, a couple of tables, and plenty of completed pilanimals.

Does it provide you room to grow?

They were only planning to set up two sewing stations at first, along with the pattern-cutting table and a filling table. As they grew, they'd need to add more sewing stations, and they had allotted enough room for that.

Is it laid out in a way that suits your needs?

Once they had graphed the way they would set up the business in this unit, they realized it was laid out quite well for their needs.

Does the property have features you'll need?

The overhead door and truck access in the back were perfect for their business, and the utilities were more than adequate.

What modifications will you need to make?

They would need to construct walls and further assemble the office and the reception area.

What repairs would be necessary?

None.

Is parking sufficient for your needs?

Yes.

Are there safety considerations?

None that don't exist everywhere.

Is the appearance of the property consistent with the image you want to portray?

Yes.

After answering these questions, Duncan and Denise decided that, if they could work out an acceptable lease agreement, they'd take it.

Chapter Nine

To Lease or Not to Lease?

Getting a start-up loan or expansion capital can be a significant challenge for the small-business owner. No matter how excited you are about your company's future, no matter how sure you are of your business's success, there will be plenty of people ready to tell you no when it comes to money.

My grandfather had a saying. "Bankers are an interesting breed. They're happy to lend you an umbrella on a sunny day, but they want it back as soon as it starts raining." I've certainly found this to be true. Banks line up to lend me money today, but back when I was new in Portland, Oregon, and just starting Sylvan Learning Centers, back when I could really have used a small loan, these same banks turned me away time and time again.

"You have no local credit history," they told me.

"I have great credit in Southern California. Check my references."

"You don't have a job."

"Of course I have a job. I'm the CEO of Sylvan Learning Centers. I'm also Sylvan's chief instructor, curriculum development manager, marketing director, bookkeeper, and I have about a dozen other jobs as well."

"Well, no one has done what you're proposing."

It kind of makes you wonder how anyone with an original idea ever got a loan. I certainly couldn't convince any of those banks to give me one, and after several frustrating days of trying, I was all but ready to give up on my business. I was short $7,500 to buy office equipment and learning materials, and I didn't see any way that I was going to be able raise that money.

A couple of days later I had lunch with a friend, Jim Monroe, who runs an ink manufacturing company in Portland. He noticed I wasn't my usual jovial self and asked me what was wrong. I explained about my disappointments with the banks and that I wasn't sure how I was going to open Sylvan without a loan.

"Most of the equipment we use at my company is leased," Jim said. "Have you ever considered leasing?"

After lunch I stopped at the telephone booth outside the restaurant and found an ad for IFG Leasing in the yellow pages. I called the local office, and, partly because it was during the lunch hour and partly because I'm lucky sometimes, the branch manager answered the phone. I explained my vision for Sylvan and my need for office equipment. My luck held up as it turned out he had a son who needed my help.

IFG wrote the lease, and my vision was back on track. Eighteen months later, when I began franchising, IFG wrote leases for several Sylvan franchisees. That first lease had resulted in a lucrative situation for both of us.

I chose to lease because there just didn't seem to be any other way. There are other reasons you might consider, though. Most small businesses just getting started have limited capital. Even if you have enough money to buy your equipment or facilities, that money might be better spent on product development, on generating goods or services that you can sell, on marketing, or simply hold it in reserve. If you are considering purchasing equipment or facilities on credit or with a loan, keep in mind that too much debt can limit other financial options.

There are many advantages to leasing, but along with the advantages come some disadvantages. Let's look at both:

Advantages

Leasing requires a smaller initial investment than purchasing. You can obtain use of the asset you need without compromising your financial position.

You may find a lessor more flexible in negotiating a payment schedule than a seller. Lease payments can be spread over a longer period of time, allowing for lower payments.

The cost of the lease is tax deductible as an operating expense.

You may have an easier time meeting the financial requirements for leasing. Banks and other lenders are usually more stringent than lessors.

Disadvantages

In the long term, leasing will often cost more than purchasing.

Too long a lease term can leave you making payments on obsolete equipment. This is particularly true for high-technology equipment.

By not purchasing, you give up the tax benefit of depreciation, effectively cancelling out the tax advantage of leasing.

While completing the terms of a lease will establish credit for your business, it may not carry the weight with creditors that successfully repaying a loan will.

Advantages	Disadvantages
Depending on the terms of the lease, the lessor may be responsible for maintenance and repairs, thereby decreasing your operating expenses.	When a real estate lease expires and is not renewed, you will cease to realize any benefit for improvements you made to the property.
You won't be stuck with obsolete equipment. When the lease expires, you are free to lease or purchase new equipment.	You don't build equity when leasing unless the lease contains a purchase option. Of course, if you exercise this option, you give up the advantage of not owning the old equipment.

Equipment Leases

The two most obvious considerations when contemplating the lease of equipment are the amount of the payment and the length of the lease, but there are several other variations of which you should be aware. Here are the main ones you will want to consider:

- K Does the lessee commit to purchase the equipment when the lease expires, have the option to purchase, or neither?
- K Who will hold title to the equipment and thereby enjoy the tax benefits during the lease?
- K Who will be responsible for maintenance, insurance, and taxes on the equipment?
- K Is there a provision for early release from the lease? Is there a penalty?

There are many factors that affect what kind of lease is right for your business. The projected value of the equipment at the end of the lease, for instance, will influence whether it's in your interest to agree to purchase the equipment or at least maintain that option. Your growth projections may affect the length of lease you are willing to commit to. These and other factors that are specific to your business will need to be considered when negotiating leases.

Now let me offer some advice on making the decision to acquire equipment. In the chapter on site selection, I suggested that you should consult your sales and expense projections when evaluating a potential location. This would be helpful, I said, in determining whether the expense of the site was in line with what you had budgeted when you evaluated the financial viability of your company. This same approach should be taken for equipment acquisition. When you develop your projections, you'll determine what equipment your business needs. You will then figure the expense for this equipment into either your start-up costs or your expected monthly expenses, depending on whether you intend to buy or to lease.

If you are considering the initial acquisition of equipment as you start a new business, you'll need to consider whether the expense will be in keeping with your projections. If they are not, you may need to recalculate based on the greater expense. Can your business afford the added monthly expense or greater start-up costs?

If you have an established business and are considering upgrading or adding equipment, you should take a slightly different approach. First you'll need to ask yourself two questions: 1) What will the business's additional monthly expenses be? 2) What will the difference be between the business's monthly income with and without the new equipment? It may be that you are buying the new equipment to increase sales or productivity. It may also be that your old equipment is no longer adequate, and not replacing it could result in a decrease in sales or productivity. Once you have made these projections, evaluate your income statement. Will the acquisition of the new equipment increase your profitability? Will not acquiring the new equipment decrease your profitability through lost productivity?

The bottom line will usually be the determining factor in decisions concerning equipment acquisition, although there may at times be other considerations. New industry regulations may require you to upgrade equipment. Environmental concerns have already forced many manufacturers to make investments that compromised their viability. A government safety inspection might also result in a your being compelled to make capital improvements that might not be made if profitability were the only concern.

Real Estate Leases

There are five basic categories of real estate leases you should be familiar with:

- K Flat Lease
- K Step Lease
- K Net Lease
- K Cost-of-living lease
- K Percentage lease

A flat lease is the simplest form of lease. The lessee agrees to pay a fixed rent throughout the life of the lease. Flat leases are not easy to find anymore. They are generally not to the lessor's advantage as the lessor's real income from the property effectively drops with inflation.

A step lease differs from a flat lease in that a step lease second guesses inflation by setting a schedule of set rent increases. During the first year of a lease, the rent might be $1000 a month. At the beginning of the second year, the rent might increase to $1050, and then to $1100 at the beginning of the third year.

A net lease eliminates the need to estimate the inflation rate over the life of the lease by attaching the rent to specific costs incurred by the lessor. There are several kinds of net leases. Some net leases base rent increases on tax increases. Others include insurance premiums in addition to taxes as a factor. A third kind of net lease attaches the rent to taxes, insurance, and maintenance costs. One concern you should have about this kind of plan is that if you, the tenant, are paying maintenance costs, there is no incentive for the lessor to keep these costs down.

A cost-of-living lease attaches the rent to the Cost of Living Index rather than to specific expenses. This kind of lease presents less risk to the lessee than a net lease as it eliminates the potential for unexpectedly large tax increases caused by reappraisal of the property, large insurance premium increases, and uncontrolled maintenance costs.

A percentage lease sets a minimum rent to be paid and adds a percentage of the business's gross income. This kind of lease is common for retail businesses in prime locations such as malls and shopping centers. Percentage leases are most beneficial to the lessor. They do, however, offer some benefits to the lessee. In the event that the business performs poorly, the lessee is protected from paying the substantial rent that would likely be required for a prime location with a different kind of lease. There is, however, often a clause in a percentage lease that allows the lessor to cancel the lease if the lessee does not generate a specified amount of income. Another benefit of a percentage lease to the lessee is that by attaching the rent to the performance of the lessee's business, it provides incentive to the lessor to maintain the property and to provide whatever assistance is possible in attracting customers.

Small-business owners are often attracted to short term leases because they are more comfortable with the shorter commitment. But longer term leases can protect the lessee as well as the lessor. Suppose you sign a one-year lease with favorable terms and open a business on a particular piece of property. You do well, and at the end of the year the lessor asks for a considerable increase in rent. The cost of moving your business may be prohibitive. You may find yourself in a poor bargaining position with few options.

One last thing about leasing, and this applies to both equipment and real estate: Never be afraid to negotiate. Whenever I approach any kind of contract, I do so with the belief that it is possible to work out a better deal, not just for me (although that's usually my main concern), but for the other party as well. Suppose a proposed equipment lease designates that the lessor will be responsible for equipment maintenance. By offering to assume this liability, you may enable yourself to negotiate a lower rent and put your business in an better financial position overall, particularly if the maintenance costs are not expected to be high. But this might also be a benefit to the lessor by eliminating both the risk and inconvenience that are associated with maintenance. Be creative when suggesting addenda to a lease. There's no telling what kind of deal you might be able to strike.

K   K   K   K

The property management company that managed the complex with the unit Duncan and Denise were interested in proposed a step lease. The rent would be $750 a month during the first year. That would increase to $770 the second year and to $790 the third and final year of the lease.

Denise tried to negotiate a flat lease—$750 a month for the entire three years—and even offered to sign a longer lease in return for better terms. The representative for the property management company explained that it wasn't up to them, that their client wouldn't budge on the rent.

"How long has the property been vacant?" Denise asked.

"About five months."

"Suppose you give us the first six months rent free, and we'll sign a lease for three years from that point on. It beats leaving the place empty."

"I'll have to check with my boss."

A couple of days later, Denise received a call. They offered her the first *three* months free with a three year lease that started after the three months were up. Denise consulted with Duncan and accepted the lease. Not only did Denise's negotiating skill get them three months free, the deal also had the effect of pushing back three months the date when they would be hit with their first rent increase.

Go Team!
Human Resources

"Employees are a company's most important resource." It's become a cliché, a line often tossed around at employee meetings when the boss feels the need to "pump up the troops." If you've ever been an employee, and most of us have, you probably know how the speech goes: "*You* are our company's most valuable asset. It is *you* who have been responsible for our success so far. And *you* will make the difference in our future success or failure. So let's get out there and win one for the CEO."

You've heard it all before, and maybe you've come to view it as strictly a motivational tool, but, cliché or not, and despite how your old boss might have used it, I believe it's true: employees are a company's most important resource. I believe this for two reasons.

First, and most obviously, employees are important because they ultimately control everything. There's not a single function in your business where success or failure is not ultimately determined by the performance of a human being. Everything hinges on your employees. It doesn't matter how good the raw materials are if they aren't correctly processed. It doesn't matter how efficient the equipment is if it isn't properly maintained. It doesn't matter how perfect the product is if it isn't effectively marketed. And it doesn't matter what a company's gross profit is if the finances aren't appropriately managed. Regardless of the quality of any other element of a company, suitable employees are necessary to the business's success. With the right human resources, even a poorly fashioned business based on a mediocre idea has a chance to succeed. But without the right human resources, even a well-conceived business founded on the most innovative idea is destined for failure. People make the difference.

The second factor that makes finding appropriate employees so important is that employees are a company's most *variable* resource. Let me explain what I mean by that.

People are complex and unpredictable, more so than anything else we have to deal with, not just in business, but in everything we do. I suppose that's what makes us interesting, but it also makes us difficult to evaluate. You can't know for sure whether a new employee will be able to adequately perform assigned duties, how that employee will react to the unique stress and pressures of a particular position, or in what way the employee will influence the existing dynamic in the work place. These are all important factors to your business, factors that can determine your profitability, factors that can make the difference between the success of your business or its failure. The scary thing is that none of these factors can be predicted with absolute certainty. You can never know for sure. Most employers have at one time or another been pleasantly surprised by employees they almost didn't hire, employees they now think they couldn't live without. And just as often they have been painfully disappointed by those they had high hopes for, but who, for one reason or another, just didn't work out.

Other resources are much more easily evaluated and obtained than human resources. A manufacturer can purchase what he believes is the appropriate quality of material for his needs, and, if he finds the material inadequate, he can order a higher grade. Once he settles on a satisfactory quality, the issue is resolved for as long as that quality of material remains affordably available or until the company's needs change. The same is true for most other resources. Everything from a company's location, its manufacturing equipment, and its accounting systems all the way down to paper clips and memo pads can be evaluated for their effectiveness and replaced or upgraded when necessary (assuming sufficient capital), and more of the same can usually be obtained as needed.

That's not the case with human resources, though. You might be able to determine that a position needs to be filled by an individual with specific training or particular skills or that an employee should have certain traits or characteristics in order to function effectively in a particular position, but those things alone won't guarantee success. There are too many variables, too many unknowns. And when you do find an employee who meets your needs, you can't turn around and order a dozen more just like her. We may joke and ask if she doesn't have a sister, but it's not that easy. People are one of a kind; no two are alike. This is why human resources are so important. This is why it is essential that you approach human resource management with thoughtful and practical systems in place, systems designed to give you the best chance to fill your personnel needs with suitable employees.

I have divided the elements of human resource management into three categories: staffing, training and development, and personnel records. Staffing consists of everything that leads up to the point at which an employee is hired. This includes determining what positions are necessary, developing job descriptions, appropriating money for salaries, recruiting, and the selection process. The selection process involves the application form, interviews, reference checks, and tests and medical exams.

Training and development deals with everything that happens once an employee has been hired, everything that you as an employer do to compensate, support, and manage the employee. This includes determining and negotiating salaries and benefits, probationary periods, job orientation, employment policies, training, supervision, and evaluations. Finally, personnel records deals primarily individual employee files, including payroll deduction information and employee evaluations.

Each of the next three chapters will be devoted to one of these three categories of human resource management. I'll discuss the specifics of each element, help you to develop appropriate systems, and make some suggestions that I think will help you handle certain situations you're likely to encounter. Then we'll take a look at Duncan and Denise to see how they apply these human resource principles to the Pilanimal business.

Chapter Eleven

Building the Team: Staffing

I have a friend, an electrician, who owns his own company. Most of Jack's business comes in the form of wiring new commercial and residential construction, but he also runs a small retail store. Why not, he figured. He doesn't get much remodel work anymore because everyone seems to be doing it themselves, he spends most of the day at the shop while his employees are out on jobs, and he has to maintain an inventory of supplies anyway. Why not pick up a few extra bucks selling to do-it-yourselfers? So he converted the front of his shop into a store, put up a sign, and hired a high school student to price merchandise, stock shelves, and do some selling after school.

Jack did better with the retail store than he'd expected and soon found he was spending more time than he could afford waiting on customers. He found himself neglecting his other duties, falling behind on paperwork, and not following up on jobs and job leads the way he previously had. So he decided he needed a store manager.

For the next couple of weeks, Jack thought about the new position as he continued to manage the store himself, but he just never got around to doing anything about it. Then one

73

afternoon a man came in looking for work and said he used to work in the electrical department of a large chain hardware store. Jack hired him on the spot. Well, things didn't work out very well. Jack's new employee was always late for work, they could never agree on what the responsibilities of a store manager should include, and, on top of it all, the guy wasn't happy with his salary after his first month.

"What did I do wrong?" Jack asked me when he told me the story. "What should I have done differently?"

There are five basic elements in the hiring or *staffing* process, five basic steps that an employer should take before making a hiring decision. Jack completed *only* one of them: he identified a need. I agree with him that a store manager is a necessary position for his business, but once he'd made that determination, there were four more steps he should have taken, four elements of staffing that could have helped him avoid a situation that would end up adversely affecting his business.

After deciding to hire a store manager, Jack should have developed a job description for the position. He should have appropriated a certain amount of money to compensate the position, systematically recruited for the position, and conducted a selection process of interviews and reference checks. Any of these steps might have saved Jack from some of the difficulties he encountered with his new employee. Let's look at each element a little more closely.

Determine what positions are necessary

Jack was able to do this, but a lot of small-business owners have a hard time with it. Some simply refuse to turn over even the least bit of responsibility to anyone else. They live and die by the motto: if you want something done right, do it yourself. Others seem to hire someone new every time they turn around.

Obviously neither extreme is in your company's best interest, but even the shrewdest, most discerning entrepreneurs have difficulty knowing what positions will significantly advance the mission of their business and which are marginal. I'm regularly asked, "Berry, how do I know when I should hire?"

The best advice I can give is to go back to your mission statement. Use it to evaluate the creation of this new position. Ask yourself, "Will creating this position advance the mission of my company?" Try to picture the right employee in the position and envision the results. What problems are solved? What opportunities are created? How does this affect your mission? There may not always be easy answers, but at least you're asking the right questions.

Develop a job description

It is absolutely essential that you define the duties and responsibilities of all company positions. First, it's only fair to employees. They have a right to know exactly what is expected of them. How else are they going to have a chance to succeed? Second, *you* need to have the duties and responsibilities clearly defined in order to determine what qualifications to look for in recruits and applicants.

Here are the elements I suggest you include in a job description. Start with the job title. This doesn't have to be fancy. Salesperson, Maintenance Person, and Accounting Clerk are all perfectly fine job titles. I think it's important, though, that you and your employees know what their positions are with the company, and that starts with a title.

After the job title, I like to include a purpose or summary statement. You might think of this as a mini-mission statement for the job. Approach the purpose statement the same way you did your mission statement. Ask yourself similar questions. What's this position all about? And what do I hope to accomplish by creating this position? A position's purpose statement, like your company's mission statement, can help the employee keep sight of the bigger picture. It's something an employee can come back to when discouraged or bogged down by the pressures and stress of everyday operations. And, along with the job title, it gives the employee an identity within the company.

A sales position's purpose statement might be "To sell the company's products through prompt and courteous attention to the customer's needs." A maintenance position's purpose statement might be "To maintain all company property for its most efficient use in advancing the company's mission." Purpose statements don't need to be elaborate. They should clear and concise expressions of purpose, using direct and understandable language.

After the statement of purpose, a job description should identify the employee's supervisor. This may be you, or perhaps you have a manager, but the employee needs to know who will be evaluating his performance and whom he should ask for direction. The issue of supervision is also important to you. In order to maintain efficiency, it is essential that you have a hierarchy in place. I've seen too many situations where an employee gets contradictory directions from two bosses. The employee becomes frustrated and progress is hindered.

Next you should include a list of duties and responsibilities. This is the heart of the job description. Make a list of everything the position involves. Then try to reduce the list to a set of clearly defined duties and responsibilities. Duties should be specific enough that a supervisor is able to objectively evaluate and communicate to the employee whether responsibilities are being satisfactorily met, but not so detailed as to require revision with every minor change in the company's needs.

Suppose a small retail store wanted to hire someone to do some cleaning. "Perform needed janitorial work" is too vague. My idea of what's needed may be a lot different from yours. "Empty all garbage cans once a week" is more detailed than necessary. What happens when business picks up and the garbage cans start filling daily? "Empty garbage cans regularly" is a practical and sufficient way to word this duty. It's specific enough that the employee knows what's expected, but not so precise that it soon becomes outdated.

When you have developed a list of duties and responsibilities, evaluate each one in terms of the purpose statement you wrote. Does it advance the purpose of the position? If not, you may want to reconsider it. Or you might decide to rewrite the purpose statement. You may even find that you are actually looking for an employee to perform two separate jobs. That's OK. Write job descriptions for each and then determine how the new employee's time should be divided between these two positions.

Finally, once you've completed writing the duties and responsibilities for the job, you need to consider what qualifications you'll be looking for in an applicant. Some of these job qualifications may be quite subjective. Others will be very specific.

If you're hiring an assistant to work at a veterinary clinic, one of the qualifications might be "Must love animals." How do you verify that? They don't give a degree in it, and references would be difficult to check, but that doesn't mean you leave it out. If you think it's important, then you should document it by including it in the job description.

Other qualifications will be a bit more objective. You may require certain technical training for a position that includes the operation of machinery. Perhaps you require or prefer a certain amount of experience in your applicant. In some situations, there may be legal qualifications for a position. A bartender may need to be a certain age. A delivery driver may need a commercial driver's license. These things should all be included in the job qualifications so there's no confusion about what is required. Another important reason to list these qualifications is that they will keep you as an employer focused on what you're looking for in an employee.

Appropriate money to compensate the position

Before you start recruiting potential employees, you should have an idea of what reasonable compensation should be. This should be based on what comparable positions in your area pay. How do you find that out? Ask businesses that are similar to yours. It will help if you have some kind of relationship established with the owner or manager of the company. And you don't need to know specifics. Ask them for a salary range and what general benefits they provide.

When you get to the point of offering an applicant a job, you can work out the details of the compensation package based on the individual merits of that applicant. Perhaps you'll negotiate these with the potential employee. At this point, though, what's important is that you have an estimate of what the position is going to cost.

Recruit potential employees

There are a number of different resources you can use for recruitment. There are public employment services that will post job notices and direct applicants to you at no charge. There are private employment agencies that will recruit and screen applicants for a fee. You may decide to place an ad in the classified section of a newspaper or trade journal. If you place an ad, be as concise as possible, but make sure to adequately identify the job and its requirements so as to attract only qualified applicants. Colleges and technical schools have placement offices that will attempt to match qualified graduates to your job openings. Trade unions can be a source for skilled laborers such as plumbers or electricians. And perhaps the best way to recruit is through networking. Friends, family, people you went to school with, and anyone else you know might be able to direct you to someone who could be a perfect fit for your company.

The Selection Process

The selection process includes everything that you do to decide which, if any, of the applicants you will hire to fill the position. This begins with the application form and involves interviews, reference checks, and tests and medical exams.

Application Forms

Application forms can be purchased at most office supply stores, they can be printed for you by a professional printer, or you can design your own with any computer word processing or desktop publishing program. Many company's will find the generic forms adequate for their needs. But if you develop your own, you can customize them to your business, requesting information specific to your business. This kind of information will prove useful when sorting through the applications to determine which applicants you want to interview.

A note of caution, though: if you choose to design your own application forms, be mindful of discrimination laws. Following are lists of questions you may and may not ask on an application or in an interview:

You may ask:

- **K** Have you ever used a different last name?
- **K** Where is your residence?
- **K** Can you show legal proof of age if hired?
- **K** Are you at least 19 years old?
- **K** Can you prove you have a legal right to work in the US if hired?
- **K** What languages are you fluent in?
- **K** What is the address of your parent or guardian? (If the applicant is a minor)
- **K** Would any physical condition prevent you from performing your job?
- **K** Have you ever been convicted of a felony?
- **K** Do you belong to any professional organizations?

You may not ask:

- **K** What is your maiden name?
- **K** Do you rent or own your home?
- **K** What is your date of birth? What is your age?
- **K** When did you graduate from high school?
- **K** Are you a citizen of the United States?
- **K** Where is your birthplace? Your parents' birthplaces?
- **K** What is your native language?
- **K** Whom do you live with?
- **K** What is your marital status?
- **K** What is the occupation of your spouse?
- **K** How many children do you have? What are their ages?
- **K** Have you made arraingments for child care?
- **K** What is your race?
- **K** What is your height and weight?

K Do you have any physical disabilities?

K Have you ever filed a Worker's Compensation claim?

K What is your religious preference?

K Have you ever been arrested?

K What dates did you serve in the military? What type of discharge did you receive?

K What organizations or clubs do you belong to?

The Interview

This is a chance for you to get to know the applicant and also for the applicant to get to know you. Keep in mind that the interview is going to shape the way at least one person views your company, and perhaps a whole lot more. An interview is more than just a fact-finding endeavor. It's also a public relations opportunity. Treat applicants the same way you treat customers. Be punctual, courteous, and let them know your decision whether you hire them or not.

Your primary goal for the interview, however, is to gather information with which you'll eventually make a hiring decision. To do this, you must be prepared. Before the interview, you should decide what information you will need to learn. You should review the job qualifications set out in the job description, and you should consider what characteristics you want in all your employees. Is he dependable? Does she work well with others? Look over the application to learn what you can. Then prepare some interview questions.

During the interview, try not to monopolize the conversation. Ask questions that require thoughtful answers and then *let the applicant talk*. Try to make the applicant feel at ease. Be professional and friendly. You'll learn more from a comfortable applicant than you will from one who's feeling the pressure.

References

References often go unchecked. Don't make that mistake. References can be an important source of information, and they are as easy a picking up the telephone. Call all listed references as well as former employers. Most are happy to oblige you as long as you keep the conversation relatively short. Ask about any specific concerns you may have after the interview, and ask general questions that allow the reference giver to volunteer information about issues you may not have considered. And when talking with former employers, verify the information on the application. Chances are everything will check out, but if it doesn't, now is the time you want to know about it.

Tests and Medical Exams

Some situations may call for tests or medical exams. If a position requires working with figures, you may want to administer a mathematics test. Some companies also conduct personality tests designed to evaluate character traits such as honesty and loyalty. Personally, I tend to trust my instincts about a person based on what I learn from an interview more than how they answer a bunch of multiple choice questions, but it may be something you'll want to consider.

For a position that poses health risks to those who aren't in good physical condition, a physical exam might be appropriate. If you employ commercial drivers, you are legally required to institute or participate in a drug and alcohol testing program. You may also decide to test all employees who perform safety-sensitive tasks or all employees regardless of their positions for drugs and alcohol. But be aware that you are legally prohibited from requiring medical exams or drug and alcohol tests as part of the application process. You may require these tests as a condition of employment, but only after employment has been offered to the applicant.

Now you've gathered all the information, and it's time to decide. I suggest you review your company's mission statement and the position's purpose statement one more time. These are good things to have fresh in your mind when making such an important decision.

K K K K

Duncan and Denise decided they needed three employees: a bookkeeper/receptionist, a sewing machine operator, and a multi-duty production worker who would rotate between the pattern-cutting table, a sewing station, and the filling table. The rest of the tasks of the business—the marketing, order taking, shipping, and everything else—would be handled by Duncan and Denise. Let's follow Duncan through the steps I outlined in this chapter as they prepare to hire the production worker.

Determine what positions are necessary

Duncan and Denise had already done this. Based on their projections, they knew they needed somebody to fill this position.

Develop a job description

See the job description Duncan developed for this position on page 84.

Appropriate money to compensate the position

Because Denise had worked as a seamstress, she had some idea what they might have to pay. But after Duncan contacted a clothing manufacturer in a nearby city and a couple of other

Job Description

Job Title:
Production Worker

Purpose Statement:
To support the efficient production of the company's products

Position Supervisor:
Denise

Duties and Responsibilities:
Cut pieces for Pilanimals using patterns
Sew pieces together to assemble Pilanimals
Fill Pilanimals with polyester fiberfill
Sew closed fill-hole on Pilanimals
Maintain clean work environment
Assist with packaging and shipping
Assist with receiving

Qualifications:
Proficient with sewing machine
Dependable
Self-motivated
Able to perform same task over and over
Experience in manufacturing preferred

manufacturing companies, he realized that they wouldn't have to pay this employee as much as Denise had been making at the department store. Duncan set the monthly salary range for this position at $1200 to $1600.

Recruit potential employees

Duncan decided to begin recruiting by running an ad in the local newspaper. As it turned out, he got plenty of responses. In fact, in retrospect he says that he would think twice about using the newspaper again because he got too many responses. And if he did use the newspaper next time, he'd make sure to use a blind P.O. box.

Application Forms

Although Duncan planned to develop his own form, it wasn't high on his priority list, and he ended up using a generic form he bought at an office supply store. He used the completed applications to select the applicants he wanted to interview. Judging the applications, particularly with the generic form, proved more difficult than Duncan had imagined. After eliminating those who had no experience, Duncan was still left with 23, more than he cared to interview. He selected ten to interview first, but kept the other applications in case none of the ten worked out.

The Interview

Duncan began each interview by showing the applicant a Pilanimal and explaining the history of the company and his vision for its future. He shared the company's mission statement and discussed the job description. Then he asked the applicant questions he'd prepared. He asked each about performing the same job over and over, about how they kept motivated when the job became monotonous. He asked the applicants about their goals and ambitions. And he asked about experience with children's or health-care products.

References

After the interviews, Duncan had narrowed his choices to three. He called every reference for each of the three. Two of the applicants got rave reviews from everyone. Nobody said anything bad about the third, but Duncan felt as though a couple of the references were hedging, holding back on him. He reduced his list to two, Greg and Ruth.

Tests and Medical Exams

No tests or medical exams seemed appropriate, so Duncan decided to solicit Denise's help. She agreed to interview the two applicants. Denise interviewed each applicant in the work area. During the interview, she demonstrated how to sew a Pilanimal and then asked the applicant to repeat it for her. After watching each applicant, Denise said her decision was easy. "Hire them both," she told Duncan, "Greg as the sewing machine operator and Ruth as the production worker."

Chapter Twelve

Coaching the Team: Training and Development

So you've made a decision, hired an employee, become a boss. Now what? Most of your responsibilities as an employer fall into one of three categories. You need to compensate, support, and manage your employees. In other words, you need to pay them, provide them with the tools they need to succeed, and give them proper supervision. Each of these is a necessity if you want to have effective employees. The better and more fairly you perform your responsibilities, the more productive your employees will be for you.

Compensation

The first thing that needs to be addressed once you hire an employee is compensation. When you created the position, you developed an idea of what the position should pay. Now you need to determine the specifics. How you go about doing this will depend in part on the position and on the individual you hired. If you hired for an unskilled or semi-skilled job where all the top candidates had similar qualifications, you can pretty much determine the compensation on your own as long as it's reasonable. But if you hired an employee with special or exceptional skills, you may have to negotiate to come up with a compensation package that is acceptable to both parties.

When we talk about a compensation package, we're referring to everything that benefits the employee. This extends far beyond salary and obvious benefits like insurance and bonuses. Here's a list of the more common compensation items. You certainly won't include all these in your compensation packages; most small businesses are able to offer only a few.

- Salary and Wages
- Commissions
- Insurance
    - Health Insurance
        - Medical Insurance
        - Dental Insurance
        - Optical Insurance
    - Worker's Compensation Insurance
    - Social Security Insurance
    - Life Insurance
    - Accident Insurance
- Bonuses
    - Performance Bonuses
    - Year-end (Christmas) Bonuses
- Paid Time Off
    - Vacation
    - Holidays
    - Sick Days
- Severance Pay
- Profit-sharing Plan
- Pension Plan
- Employee Discounts

K Company Car
K Employee Lunchroom
K Company Supplied Employee Uniforms

This list is far from comprehensive. Anything you and your employee agree on can be compensation. There are two required items, though. Social Security and Worker's Compensation Insurance are government-administered programs; you are required to pay a portion of the premiums and withhold the rest from the employee's paycheck. Beyond that it's up to you.

When offering a compensation plan to an employee, make sure to discuss all the benefits. You want the employee to understand all the advantages of working for you. You will also want to be very clear about some of the benefits you do *not* offer. You don't want to exhaust your budget for a position only to have the employee come back to you and ask, "OK, now what about paid holidays."

Support

Support involves everything you do to equip your employees to succeed at their jobs. This includes job orientation, an employee handbook, and training. Too often small businesses neglect to properly support their employees. The reasons for this may be that the employer believes the employee is already fully equipped, doesn't think the company can afford to invest in employee training, or just doesn't know how to support the employee. Even if an employee is already highly trained, there will be aspects of the job unique to your company that can be learned only from you. The fact is you can't afford not to provide training and other support. Your business has a vested interest in your employees, and you should do everything possible to enhance their chances for success. After all, their success is your success.

Job Orientation

Employee support begins with job orientation. This can be informal if you choose, but there are a few things that you will want to accomplish. You want to acquaint the new employee with the company and the position, to make the employee feel comfortable, and to help the employee understand how important the job is to the company's success. But first have the new employee complete the necessary paperwork. You'll learn what that entails in the following chapter, which covers personnel records.

Then begin by sharing some of the company's history. You may want to share some of your own vision. You will definitely want to share the company's mission statement. It is essential that the employee understand the goals of the company. Encourage him to become familiar with, perhaps even memorize, the mission statement and remember it as he performs the various functions of his job.

Next examine the job description with the employee. Discuss each duty and responsibility to make sure he understands exactly what is expected. Ask him to treat the position's purpose statement with the same attention as the company's mission statement. These two statements identify his reason for being with the company.

Then take the new employee on a tour of the company's facilities. As you show him around, explain to him briefly about each area of your business to help him understand how his position relates to the whole. Introduce him to the company's other employees. Show him the employee lunch area, the rest rooms, where he should park his car, how he should record his time, and anything else he may need to know.

Employee Handbook

At some point during the job orientation, you should provide the new employee with an employee handbook. The employee handbook is a written record of your employee policies, including employee responsibilities, employer responsibilities, and procedures. It should answer many of the questions an employee might have about the job and the company.

It's important to document your policies in the handbook because it makes it easier for you to hold your employees accountable for those policies. It eliminates any question of what the policies are and whether they were communicated accurately. Have new employees read through the handbook at their leisure and then have them sign a form stating that they have read and understand the policies.

You can also be held accountable for what's in the employee handbook, so have an attorney review it to ensure there aren't any violations of business or employment laws.

The Small Business Administration suggests the following table of contents for an employee handbook.

Welcome Message
History of the Company
You and Your Future
What You Will Need to Know
 Working Hours
 Reporting to Work
 "Time Clock"
 Rest Periods
 Absence from Work
 Reporting Absences
 Employment Record

Some of the items in this suggested table of contents may not apply to your business. There may be others, such as probationary employment or disciplinary procedures, that you want to add.

Training

Training is at the heart of employee support. How you train your employees will depend on their positions and the nature of your business. There are as many kinds of training and methods for doing it as there are types of jobs. I obviously won't be able to cover all the different possibilities in any kind of detail, but I will give you some general guidelines that should enable you to develop your own training programs.

Most training is simply teaching a system to an employee. Near the beginning of the book I discussed systems. A system, I said, is an "organized, coordinated, and replicable method to achieve a desired outcome." I encouraged you to develop systems for all facets of your business. Now, as you get ready to train your employees, you are going reap some of the benefits of developing those systems.

It's easy to see how systems can be developed and taught for certain duties such as running machinery or performing accounting functions, but what about some of the more subjective aspects of a job like customer courtesy? These sorts of things should be part of a training program, too. I was in a well-known home store with my wife, Annie, recently and observed what was clearly a system for customer courtesy.

"Did you find everything you were looking for today?" the young woman working the register asked my wife as we were checking out.

"I didn't find the paper towels that were advertised in the newspaper last Sunday," Annie told her.

"I can have a courtesy clerk bring them to the counter," the woman responded. "How many packages would you like?" She made the request over the intercom, and before she had finished ringing up our other purchases the paper towels had arrived.

Somebody at the company had developed a system for customer courtesy. It was organized, coordinated, and replicable. It achieved the desired outcome, and it was easy to teach. I've known business owners who have nearly gone mad trying to teach customer service. They try to communicate ideas such as "make the customer's problem your problem." They try to teach employees "goodwill" toward customers. There's nothing wrong with that, but no amount of goodwill on the part of the woman at the register would have produced results the way a simple, well-designed system did.

So far I've been discussing in-house training (that is, training done by you or someone in your company). There are also outside sources of training that you should consider. These include:

- Formal college courses
- Trade schools
- Product knowledge classes put on by vendors
- Courses offered by industry associations and private companies

Management

Finally, you must manage your employees. Employee management includes probationary periods, supervision, and evaluations. A lot of what falls into the category of employee management could also be considered support. The feedback that an employee gets during an evaluation, for instance, will presumably equip him to better perform his job. And an employee's supervisor will probably be the employee's primary source of support.

Probationary Period

When you hire an employee, it's a good idea to offer him probationary employment for a set period of time, perhaps 30 days, with the understanding that at the end of the probationary period you will evaluate his performance and decide whether to offer him regular employment. If you have concerns after the probationary period that cause you believe he is not the best person for the position, you simply do not rehire. Or if at any time during the probationary period you determine that you aren't going to rehire him, the probationary period ends and employment is terminated.

There are a couple of advantages to the probationary period. First, it is a system for evaluating new employees. It identifies a time when the evaluation will take place and a decision will be made. Without this system in place, evaluations can be delayed and forgotten. Another advantage is that it gives the employee a chance to evaluate the company and the position to determine whether they are right for him. Finally, probationary employment may help protect you from a wrongful dismissal charge in case things don't work out. You did not fire the employee; his probation ran out, and he wasn't rehired.

Supervision

In addition to a supervisor's support duties, I like to think of supervision as quality control for a job. It is the supervisor's responsibility to monitor an employee's performance, to reward outstanding performance, and to correct unsatisfactory performance. You should develop systems for each of these functions.

Systems for monitoring, rewarding, and correcting performance not only enhance efficiency but ensure that all employees are treated equally and fairly.

Evaluations

A supervisor's major system for monitoring performance is regularly scheduled evaluations. Your company may conduct formal evaluations only annually or semiannually, but you should still schedule informal evaluations at more frequent intervals.

For formal evaluations, I suggest you develop an evaluation form. To create this form, list all the duties and responsibilities from the employee's job description, leaving room to rate the employee's performance in each of these areas as well as to write comments. I use a rating scale of one to five with one representing unsatisfactory performance and five representing outstanding performance, but you can use any scale you choose. In addition to the specific duties and responsibilities for the position, list items such as dependability, ability to work with others, and attitude. At the end of the form leave room to set goals and to evaluate progress on the goals set at the last evaluation.

At the beginning of the evaluation, have the employee and the supervisor independently fill out copies of the rating portion of the evaluation form. They should then compare responses item by item, discussing any discrepancies. After reviewing the rating section together, the employee and the supervisor should agree on goals for the employee. Goals, as always, should be specific and measurable. "Sell more cars" is not measurable. "Sell five cars a month" is a better goal. The employee and the supervisor should also review goals set at the previous evaluation. Finally, the employee should be given a chance to ask questions and air complaints.

Informal evaluations can use a similar form or can be as simple as a short paragraph written by the supervisor about the employee's performance. Make sure to share all evaluations with the employee as one of the main purposes for the evaluation is to improve the employee's performance. Also, if the employee disagrees with an unfavorable evaluation, the employee should be allowed to write a dissenting statement. All evaluations and dissenting statements should be placed in the employee's file.

Disciplinary Action

You or a supervisor may determine through a scheduled evaluation or through everyday observation that an employee's performance is unsatisfactory. It may be that the employee fails to perform regular duties and responsibilities or that he has violated company policies with frequent tardies or insubordination. When this happens, the first thing you must do is attempt to determine who is at fault. Be open to the possibility that the employee might not be adequately supported. It's easy to blame the employee, but if the employee isn't at fault, that's not going to help the employee or the company. You may need to reconsider how the company supports the position.

If the employee *is* at fault, try to correct the problem informally at first. Sometimes just pointing out the problem or offering a little extra encouragement can have amazing results. However, if the poor performance continues and needs to be addressed formally, it is important that you do so in a fair and objective way.

Issue the offending employee a written disciplinary statement. The disciplinary statement should consist of four parts:

K An objective statement of the offense
K The consequence of the offense

- **K** The amount of time allowed for improvement
- **K** The probable consequence if there is not adequate improvement

Possible consequences for an offense are:

- **K** Warning
- **K** Suspension without pay
- **K** Demotion
- **K** Termination

Employees should be allowed to write a dissenting or mitigating statement, which will be placed in the employee's file along with a copy of the disciplinary statement. It is essential that you keep all these documents so that you can defend your disciplinary actions should charges be brought against you.

Performance Rewards

It's just as important to reward outstanding performance as it is to correct poor performance. It provides incentive for employees to excel. Rewards can be as simple as recognition for a job well done or can take the form of promotions, raises, bonuses, or any other award you can think of. You should recognize specific achievements in your employees such as completion of training or making a large sale for the company. You should also recognize consistent performance such as departments that regularly meet manufacturing quotas or employees that never miss work.

What's the best way to approach employee rewards? You guessed it. Develop a system. There are many ways to do this. One is to establish specific criteria for receiving awards and a procedure for applying those criteria. You might decide to give an extra Christmas bonus to any employee who doesn't miss a scheduled work day. Part of your system would include establishing a date on which you would review employee records each December to determine which employees receive the bonus.

Compensate, support, and manage your employees. If you do these three things well, and if you made good hiring decisions, you'll have crossed one of the most difficult hurdles to business success.

K K K K

Duncan called Ruth to offer her the job and set an appointment for the following day to discuss the details. When Ruth arrived for the appointment, Duncan proposed a compensation package that included a $1200 monthly salary, five paid holidays a year, a one week paid vacation after one year of employment, and a basic medical insurance package. He told her they were also considering an incentive plan that would pay employees bonuses for exceeding quotas. Duncan explained that Ruth would be hired for a probationary period of 90 days. Her performance would then be evaluated and both Ruth and the company would decide whether they wanted to continue employment. If they agreed that she would remain with the company, Ruth would receive a $50 a month raise. Ruth accepted the job on those terms and agreed to begin the following Monday.

Ruth arrived just before eight o'clock Monday morning. Duncan reintroduced her to Denise, who would be Ruth's supervisor. Denise and Ruth were soon joined by Greg. Denise showed them both how to record their time and gave them a more detailed explanation of Pilanimals, Inc. than Duncan had shared during the interview. Denise had produced a short, employee handbook and gave a copy to each of the new employees. They spent some time going over the information, and Denise answered questions.

About mid-morning Denise began training Ruth and Greg to do their jobs. Ruth was to cut all the pieces out of the appropriate colors and weights of nylon fabric for the Pilanimals they were producing that day. (At this point the company was producing six different "species" of Pilanimals, but we'll explain how that came about when we get to marketing.) Greg then sewed the major pieces together. Denise added the detail pieces such as the ears and noses, and then Ruth filled the Pilanimals with polyester fiberfill. One of the three, depending on who was available, would then sew up the fill holes, and the Pilanimals would go into boxes for shipping.

Chapter Thirteen

Team Stats: Personnel Records

There are several reasons to maintain personnel records. Some of the documents you keep in employee files will help you comply with government employment regulations and requirements. Others will increase your company's efficiency at employee management. And many of these records can protect you against potential liability resulting from your dealings with employees. In this chapter, I will provide you with a list of items that should be kept in an employee file. The list is divided into those records that are legally required and those that I recommend. Following the list, I will explain the items and, when appropriate, tell you where to get the necessary forms.

- **K** Required Records
  - **K** Forms
    - **K** Form I-9, Employee Eligibility Verification
    - **K** Form W-4, Withholding Allowance Certificate
    - **K** Check with the appropriate state agencies to see if there are any required forms specific to your state

K Records
  - **K** Records of wages and taxes
  - **K** Records of hours worked
- **K** Recommended Records
  - **K** Hiring Records
    - **K** Completed employment application
    - **K** Résumé (if provided)
    - **K** Letters of reference (if provided)
    - **K** Pre-employment test results (if tests were given)
    - **K** Copy of job description
    - **K** Signed statement that the employee has read and understands the policies covered in the employee handbook
  - **K** Performance Records
    - **K** Copy of evaluations
    - **K** Copy of disciplinary statements
    - **K** Copy of dissenting or mitigating statements written by the employee
    - **K** Records of commendations or awards

Form I-9, Employee Eligibility Verification, serves as verification that the employee can legally work in the United States. You must keep a completed I-9 form for each of your employees, but you should keep them in a separate file. The federal government can demand to see I-9 forms at any time, but there's no reason to give them access to all your personnel records. You can obtain blank I-9 forms from the US Immigration and Naturalization Service (INS).

Form W-4, Withholding Allowance Certificate, provides the information necessary for withholding income tax from the employee's paychecks. You can obtain W-4 forms from your local IRS office.

I-9 and W-4 forms are the two forms that the federal government requires that you keep in your records. There may be additional state or local requirements. Check with the appropriate agencies.

It is important to keep accurate records of wages paid and taxes withheld. You will need this information for certain reports you must file. It's also important to have this information documented if you are audited or in case any disputes arise over whether wages or taxes were calculated and paid correctly. Records of hours worked may also be important for settling disputes about past wages, and you will need this information when paying Worker's Compensation premiums.

You should keep all documents associated with the hiring process in an employee's personnel file. One of the main purposes of a personnel file is to create a record of the employee's history with the company, and hiring was the first event in that history. You may want to use this information when considering an employee for a promotion, or, if you discover that an employee misrepresented himself during the hiring process, you'll want to have documentation to justify yourself when you take appropriate action. The employee's signed statement that he has read and understands the policies covered in the employee handbook is particularly important. It will discredit any argument by the employee that he wasn't aware of certain company policies.

Finally, keep copies of all employee performance records in the employee file. Evaluations, disciplinary statements, and records of commendations or awards can all be useful tools when considering the employee for raises or promotions. They can also be used to substantiate a case for termination of employment or other disciplinary action. And you may want to refer to these records when giving a reference for an employee in the future.

Keeping personnel records is not difficult. Most of the items that you need to keep are documents that you will handle anyway, and the others are relatively easy to produce. It's just a matter of setting up a few file folders in a file cabinet drawer and being disciplined enough to keep it updated. It's really not much work, and it can save you a lot of time and money in the future.

K K K K

When Duncan hired Ruth, he had her fill out W-4 and I-9 forms. He put the I-9 form in a file with Greg's I-9 form. The W-4 form along with Ruth's employment application and some notes Duncan had made during their interview became the first items in Ruth's personnel file. Duncan would soon add records of wages, taxes, and hours worked, and later copies of Ruth's evaluations.

Chapter Fourteen

Inventory Control: Are We Out of That Again?

A couple of weeks ago I had lunch with my marketing director, Lana, at a small Fifties-style diner where hamburgers, fries, and milkshakes are the main fare. When Lana ordered a strawberry shake, Cliff, our waiter, apologized. "I'm afraid we can't do that today," he said. "We're out of milk."

"Out of milk? How hard can it be?" Lana asked. "There's a grocery store across the street."

"I'm sorry," Cliff said, "but we're in the middle of the noon rush, and we simply can't spare anyone for even a few minutes."

Well, Lana's a problem solver, and she really wanted that milkshake. "Tell you what," she said, "I'll go buy the milk for you." Cliff gave her money from the register, and Lana was soon back with two gallons of milk. Cliff was grateful, but Lana still had to pay for the shake.

Although this story has a relatively happy ending, it demonstrates a situation where there was breakdown in inventory control. The diner either didn't have a system in place for inventory control or their system failed. By the time Lana showed up to save the day, they had presumably already lost several milkshake sales, and probably some future sales of hamburgers and fries as well.

As a business, you work too hard and spend too much money to attract customers just to turn them away when you finally get their attention. But that's exactly what happens when you run out of inventory. And attracting them a second time will be even more difficult than the first.

There's another common mistake made in inventory control that can have equally damaging consequences. Overstocking can be just as bad as understocking. There are a couple of reasons businesses overstock. Some businesses do so as a buffer against too little inventory. Sometimes it seems easier to buy too much rather than investing the energy to figure out what the correct inventory levels should be. Other businesses buy more than they need to take advantage of quantity price breaks. While this may make sense in certain situations, it results in a larger investment in inventory, which usually means a smaller percentage return on your investment. Here's an example.

Several years ago, when I lived in California, I knew the owner of a small hardware store. Dave's company sold about 2000 gallons of paint a year, roughly 40 gallons a week, although there were certain times during the year when he could count on selling more and times when he knew the paint business would be slow.

Dave was able to purchase paint weekly from the vendor he used, but once a year in late December his vendor made a special offer. Once a year Dave could buy paint for 30% less than he could during the rest of the year. He regularly took advantage of this special buy and bought a year's supply of paint. He had to invest over $10,000 to do this, but he always considered himself a savvy businessman for what he called his "foresight."

Throughout the course of the year, Dave still had to order paint to fill in the gaps created when he sold more of a particular product than he'd projected. There were additional costs for the space the paint took up in his small warehouse, the time involved in regularly moving the paint in and out of the way, and the damage (or *shrinkage*) that invariably occurred throughout the year. Still, after considering all these factors, Dave figured he showed a gross profit of about $15,000 on paint each year.

Then one February we experienced an unusual cold spell, and much of Dave's paint was ruined when it froze in his poorly insulated warehouse. The next December Dave bought only a one month supply of paint, unwilling to risk such a large loss again. Here's what he found over the next year.

His gross profit on paint wasn't quite as high as when he bought it on special, but after accounting for the storage and shrinkage costs he did not incur, it wasn't that much less either. Where he had grossed around $15,000 in previous years, he now grossed just over $13,000. But what had never occurred to him before was that by buying only enough paint at a time to be adequately stocked for a few weeks, he never had much more than $1,000 invested, even during his busy seasons.

Now you tell me, which is preferable?

A) Make an investment of $10,000 and earn a $15,000 profit over the course of a year
B) Keep $1,000 invested for a year and make $13,000

Dave decided the answer was "B," and Dave was right.

What can we learn from Lana's diner incident and Dave's paint situation? *The challenge of inventory control is to efficiently maintain an adequate quantity and quality of inventory with the least investment.* The systems you develop for this will depend largely on factors such as what you do with your inventory, how you obtain your inventory, and the predictability of your need for inventory. Let's look at these factors.

There are three basic things a business may do with inventory, three basic categories that inventory falls into:

K Raw Materials
K Merchandise
K Service Supplies

Raw materials are anything that will be processed into merchandise. This includes cloth for a tailor, flour for a baker, and wood for a furniture maker. Merchandise is anything a business intends to sell. Merchandise includes everything found on the shelves of retail stores, such as groceries, clothes, or televisions, and everything sitting in manufacturers' or distributors' warehouses waiting to be sold, such as plywood at a mill or steel at a refinery. Service supplies are those things used in performing services. Service supplies include glass cleaner for a cleaning service, shampoo at a hair salon, and fertilizer for a lawn care service.

Inventory is obtained in one of two ways:

K It is purchased
K It is processed from raw materials

Processing doesn't always involve manufacturing in the way we normally think of it. A wheat farmer might be said to process seed into a crop. A logging company obtains the rights to standing timber and processes it into logs, which later may be processed into lumber.

As we have seen, being able to predict your need for inventory as accurately as possible is important. Some types of businesses will have an easier time with this than others. The inventory needs of a hot dog vendor in a park will be greatly effected by the weather, for example. Rain may slow his business to a crawl, while an unexpectedly warm weekend in early spring may mean a business boon. A hot dog vendor will have a much more difficult time predicting inventory needs than a window manufacturer who has orders four weeks in advance and knows exactly what will need to be ready and when.

There are three main systems you will need to develop for inventory control:

K A system for determining necessary inventory
K A system for obtaining inventory
K A system for tracking inventory

Let me tell you about a business with relatively simple but efficient systems for these three needs. When I arrived home from work a couple of nights ago, I noticed a pickup truck parked in my neighbor's driveway with the words "Mobile-Lube" painted on the door. I also noticed a man there changing my neighbor's oil. What a great idea, I thought. My car's oil was due to be changed, but I just never seemed to get it into a service center. So I walked next door to see if the Mobile-Lube man would be available to change my oil.

"I can make an appointment for you for anytime tomorrow," he said. "But I wouldn't have the right filter with me now."

"You don't keep an inventory in your truck?" I asked.

"I couldn't keep a filter for every vehicle I might work on," he explained. "There's just too many." It seems most of his customers set up appointments a day or two in advance, and he stops by an auto parts store each morning to pick up what he needs.

"I see you keep windshield wiper blades with you," I said. There was a board attached to the inside wall of his truck's canopy. Two packs of wiper blades hung from each of the nails that extended from the board.

"They're an add-on sale," he told me. "I try to sell them when I get to a job, so I keep a couple of packs of each kind in the truck."

Mobile-Lube had systems for determining necessary inventory, for obtaining inventory, and for tracking inventory. The system for determining necessary inventory consisted of two basic steps. First, when an oil-change appointment was made, appropriate information such as make, model, and year of the car was taken. Second, each morning the Mobile-Lube man would look over his appointments and make a list of each filter he would need that day. The system for obtaining this inventory also involved two steps. After leaving home each morning, the Mobile-Lube man drove to an auto parts store and purchased what he needed. The second step involved keeping the receipts for accounting purposes. Finally, the Mobile-Lube man had developed a system for tracking his wiper blade inventory. The board that held the blades was his system. Every nail on the board held a different kind of wiper blade. Each morning when he stopped at the auto parts store, all he had to do was glance at the board to see where his inventory levels were.

Your business probably won't be able to get by with systems as simple as those used by Mobile-Lube, but, if you're a small business with relatively little inventory, you shouldn't have to develop incredibly complicated systems either.

Finally, let me say a few words about computerized inventory control systems. This can be a great way to go. The systematic nature of inventory control lends itself to computerization. And there may be a computer program that has been specifically designed for your particular kind of business. If you own a franchise, are a member of a cooperative buying group, or buy regularly from a vendor, these are good places to start asking about computer inventory programs. You might also look to businesses that are similar to yours or to trade journals. If you don't find a program tailored to your kind of business, consider a generically designed program. The salesperson at your local computer or software store can give you advice concerning the latest inventory control software on the market.

One bit of advice, though: there are multi-function computer programs and packages that will handle several of your computer needs, from accounting to order processing to inventory control. If you can get one program that handles all your computer needs, or several programs that are designed to communicate with each other, it can save you a lot of time and frustration. Everything that goes on in your business is related to everything else, so it will be important to transfer data between programs. Whenever you sell something, it affects your inventory and necessitates an accounting task. If your computer programs automatically make these connections, it can save you from needing to figure out how to force them to do so or even from needing to re-enter the data manually for each business function it affects.

Whether or not you decide to use a computer, proper systems for inventory control are a must. Too little inventory will keep you from properly serving your customers. Too much inventory adds an unnecessary financial burden. But there's a balance in between that can help lead your business to profitability and success.

K K K K

During the first year of Pilanimal production, Denise had purchased fabric and polyester fiberfill at a local fabric store. They'd had to order the black and white nylon she was using for the panda bears, but it was still a convenient arrangement for Denise. But now that they were going to produce a lot more Pilanimals in several different species, Denise decided to explore some other means of obtaining materials. She found a fabric wholesaler who would sell her the nylon she needed for $3.75 per yard if she bought it in quantities larger than 10,000 yards, or $3.95 per yard if she bought in smaller quantities.

Denise and Duncan discussed their options. The complex they rented in had storage units available for $50 a month that could hold 10,000 yards of fabric, and the $.20 per yard savings on 10,000 yards amounted to $2000. That was tempting. But it only took about yard of fabric to make a Pilanimal, and they didn't need the materials for 10,000 Pilanimals on hand at a time. They'd also have to handle all the material an additional time if they stored it in another warehouse, not to mention paying for it all up front.

They decided they were better off keeping only about 600 yards in stock at a time. They had room to store that much under the pattern-cutting table, and it only took three days to have more fabric shipped if they ever ran low. Considering the interest they'd have to pay on the $37,500 it would cost to make the larger purchase, the storage costs, and the increased cost of handling, they'd eat up the 20¢ they'd save on each Pilanimal pretty quickly. Then they'd be left with the same amount of profit on a much larger investment. It just didn't make any sense. Duncan and Denise decided to purchase in the smaller quantities.

Chapter Fifteen

Roast Beef on Rye, Hold the Mayo: Order Processing

I've ordered enough pizza in my day to know the drill.

"May I help you?"

"I'd like to place an order."

"For pick-up or delivery?"

"Delivery."

"May I have your address, last name, and phone number, please?"

I provide this information, and the order taker asks me what I would like to order.

"A large half mushroom and olive and half cheese pizza."

"We'll have that out to you in about thirty minutes."

There are variations, of course. Sometimes they want to tell me about their special. Other times they try to sell me extra cheese. But the basic routine stays the same, and half an hour later my kids, Nickie and Billy, and I in front of the television with a Disney video and a piping hot pizza.

So what goes on between the time I place my order and when my pizza arrives? Here's what I presume happens:

As I place my order, all the information goes onto a form. There's a box to be checked for pick-up or delivery. There's a place for my name, address, and telephone number, and, of course, for my order. The form prompts the order taker to ask for all the pertinent information. Finally, the order taker prices the pizza.

Once the form is completed, it goes to the kitchen. There the pizza chef uses it to create my pizza to the proper specifications. When the pizza is ready, the delivery is assigned to one of the drivers, who uses the information from the form to find my house. My kids and I take it from there.

The pizza parlor has complete systems for order processing, and these may be the most important systems in their business. Everything they do supports order processing. Without it, there would be no reason for marketing, inventory control, or accounting. There would be no reason to have employees. There wouldn't even be a reason to have the business. Order processing is the central function of a business. It's what you get paid for. If you can't process an order correctly, you might as well close the doors and rejoin the work-a-day world of unsympathetic bosses and financial dependence. But you *can* process orders correctly. It's just a matter of developing proper systems.

If the pizza parlor didn't have systems, or if any of the systems were to break down, I might not get my pizza. Or my pizza might be wrong, which is only slightly better than not getting it at all. If they didn't have a system, the order taker might forget to ask me what kind of crust I want on my pizza. But as long as she follows the system, as long as she uses the form, she's not going to forget because the form won't let her forget. As long as the pizza chef follows the system, my pizza will be made correctly, and as long as the driver follows the system, my pizza will arrive at the right house in a timely manner and everyone will be happy.

There are three necessary systems for order processing at the pizza parlor, and they're pretty easy to identify:

K Taking the Order
K Filling the Order
K Shipping the Order

These are the same three systems your company will need. Taking the order consists of receiving an order commitment from a customer and collecting the necessary information. Filling the order involves making the order ready for the customer. This may include manufacturing, performing a service, or simply gathering the appropriate items together. Shipping or delivering the order is simply getting the filled order to the customer. This can be as involved as loading the material onto a truck and transporting it across town or as simple as handing the merchandise across a counter.

Sometimes the distinction between order filling and delivery becomes blurred. If you run a lawn care business, going to the customer's home is included in the service. It's part of your product. It's part of filling the order. If you run a delivery service, delivery is your product.

In your particular business, if distinguishing between order filling and order delivery makes it easier for you to develop systems, then observe the distinction. But if it make more sense in your business to combine the two, there's nothing wrong with that.

Taking the Order

Order taking is the foundation for order processing. Although accurate order taking won't guarantee proper results, sloppy order taking *will* lead to mistakes, possibly costly ones.

I recently did some consulting for a retail company that was opening a new 80,000 square foot store in Boise, Idaho. Like most chains, they use a particular color scheme for their stores, a color scheme that is recognizable to their customers. But when they ordered the fixtures (the shelving units) for the new store, the order taker for the company they were buying from transposed two letters. These letters designated the main and trim colors for the fixtures. The order was filled correctly, at least according to the paperwork. Some pieces had to be manufactured. Others had to be painted. And the order was shipped from the East Coast. When it arrived, the colors were backward. The order filling system and the order delivery system were executed perfectly, but they might as well not have been done at all. One little mistake, a breakdown in the order taking system, resulted in a huge expense for the fixture company and a two-week delay for the retail company.

You may not be able to eliminate every human error, but the right order taking system should help you cut down on a lot of them. Since order taking is primarily an information gathering function, you'll want to have a system that prompts the order taker to ask for every bit of necessary information. Forms work great for this, and in some cases, computers work even better. Either way, first you'll have to determine exactly what information you'll need and then develop a system that collects it.

An order taking system, while a function of order processing, can also lend itself to marketing. When I call the pizza parlor and the order taker tells me about their daily special or offers me extra cheese, that's marketing. When the person taking your order at the hamburger stand asks, "Would you like fries with that?" that's marketing, too. You may want to incorporate certain marketing devices into your order taking system. This can be encouraging add-on sales as in the pizza parlor or the hamburger stand. It also might be soliciting information that can be used in marketing. Questions like "How did you hear about us?" or "What made you decide to choose us?" can help you discover what you're doing right help and help you to develop new marketing strategies. Of course, if you decide to pursue this kind of marketing, you'll want to have a system for recording the answers to these questions and channeling the information to your marketing department.

Filling the Order

Order filling is the core of order processing. As much as anything else, being able to fill orders properly and efficiently will keep customers coming back.

The way an order is filled will depend on your business. It may be collecting and packaging merchandise for shipment, manufacturing an item, or performing a service. However you fill orders, I suggest you include in your system a method for checking to make sure all the steps have been completed. If your business is mail order, the order might come to the order filling department in the form of an invoice with all the purchased items listed. Each line of the invoice would probably have a box to check when the item was put into the shipping container and a place for an employee to sign when the entire order was filled. If you have a cleaning business, you might use a standard checklist where your employees would check off the different cleaning functions as they performed each one. In either case, the completed checklist should be returned to a supervisor. This kind of quality control in your order filling department can prevent an employee from inadvertently missing a step in the process and also gives you a starting point if a customer complains that an order was not filled properly.

Shipping the Order

Order delivery picks up where order filling leaves off. The main element of the order delivery system is to coordinate the logistics of the delivery. Some companies may want to incorporate a step into their delivery system to double check that orders are filled correctly.

When there is a breakdown in order processing, it often happens during the transition between two systems, as the order moves from order taking to order filling or from order filling to order delivery. When I placed my pizza order, if the order taker had not put the order in the right hands or placed it on the carousel between the order desk and the kitchen or whatever their system is, my pizza wouldn't have been made. And if my pizza had not passed from the kitchen to the driver, I wouldn't have received it. You should work steps into your systems that will ensure that orders don't get lost. You might choose to incorporate some kind of tracking system. You could make your order taker responsible to see that orders have been filled and delivered at the appointed time. Or you might have a supervisor who oversees all orders through the entire process. In some businesses, the order taker is also the order filler and possibly the delivery person as well. In this situation, the transition from one system to another should take less effort, but it's still a good idea to develop some kind of checking procedure to be sure that everything happens according to plan. Some customers are more understanding than others, but no one is happy when an order is lost.

Other Order Processing Systems

There are a couple of more systems that you may need to work into order processing although they are really accounting functions. Invoicing is often done when an order is taken, and collecting is often done when an order is delivered. Pizza delivery is a good example of this. When I placed my order, the order taker figured the price, and I paid the person who delivered the pizza. If these functions are going to be performed during order processing, it's important to work them into the appropriate systems. You may need steps for pricing in your order taking system, for instance. These may be as simple as taking prices from a list. Or they may involve a more complex scheme of pricing levels and quantity breaks. Either way, you'll want to make sure your employees are equipped to do it right. You may also want to include steps in one of your systems to ensure payment before delivery. A mail order business, for example, may hold delivery for an unfamiliar customer until a check clears the bank.

Whatever your order processing needs, it is important to develop efficient systems. For most businesses, proper order processing, more than anything else, will advance their mission. It's not something you want to leave to chance.

K K K K

Let's see what systems Duncan and Denise developed for each of the three steps in order processing:

Taking the Order

Duncan would be the primary order taker. Sometimes he would take orders over the phone, and sometimes he would take them when calling on potential customers. Wherever he was, he would fill out a form. The top of the form contained all the customer information: name, mailing address, shipping address, method of payment, etc. The body of the form identified the products and quantities ordered. The bottom of the form contained shipping information including method of shipment and expected shipping date. Once Duncan had completed the form he made a copy of it. He put the copy in the order box on Denise's desk and gave the original to the bookkeeper, who processed the billing information and made the appropriate accounting entries.

Filling the Order

Denise developed these simple steps for filling the order:

1. She transferred all of the order information including the shipping information from the order form to an order log. This way they never had to worry about an order getting lost.
2. She checked their completed inventory to determine how many, if any, Pilanimals had to be produced to fill the order.
3. She checked their raw materials to make sure there was enough in stock to produce the needed Pilanimals.
4. She scheduled the production on the dry erase board in the production room. She also kept a paper copy of the schedule at her desk in case the board was inadvertently erased.

The production staff—Denise, Ruth, and Greg—followed the schedule and produced the necessary Pilanimals.

Shipping the Order

Each morning, Denise looked over the order log to see what orders needed to be shipped. She called freight companies to arrange shipping a couple of days in advance, and then filled in the name of the freight company and the other pertinent information. Then she made sure all orders that were being shipped that day were properly packaged and labeled and in the area designated for shipping. And when the packages were picked up, she marked a box in the order log so that she could see at a glance which orders had been shipped and which hadn't.

With these three systems in place, Duncan and Denise felt confident that they could efficiently process orders and serve their customers promptly.

Chapter Sixteen

Risky Business: Risk Management

Everyday as I drive to work I pass a sign. It's one of those electronic signs that can be programmed to display the time and temperature, promotions, and any other information the programmer wants to share with the world. This particular sign is used to display a daily saying, a clever witticism, an inspirational adage. You know the kind of thing I'm talking about: "When you get to the end of your rope, tie a knot and hang on a little longer." "This is the first day of the rest of your life." "Remember, there is no *I* in *T-E-A-M*." Sometimes they make you smile. Sometimes you grimace.

Yesterday I grimaced. The sign read, "Life is ten percent what you make it and ninety percent how you take it." What kind of message is that? This is what they're really saying: *You can't do anything about nine out of ten of the things that affect the circumstances of your life, so the sooner you learn to accept things the way they are, the happier you'll be.*

I keep thinking somebody must have just gotten the numbers turned around. Maybe they meant to write, "Life is ninety percent what you make it and ten percent how you take it." Doesn't that make a lot more sense? It's certainly a lot closer to my own philosophy, and, if you consider yourself an entrepreneur, I hope it's closer to yours, too. Entrepreneurs don't just lie back and accept whatever happens. Entrepreneurs make things happen.

That's not to say that you can control everything, because you can't. Business, like every other aspect of life, is wrought with uncertainties, unrealized expectations, and unforeseen misfortunes. The business world is full of risks. It's how you handle those risks that will make the difference between your success and failure.

The risks of being in business can be divided into five general categories:

K Risks to the safety of your customers, your employees, yourself, and anyone else who has contact with your company: A customer may slip on a wet floor. An employee may be injured operating machinery. A delivery driver may cause an accident injuring a pedestrian.

K Risks of damage to your facilities, equipment, or inventory: Any kind of disaster—earthquake, flood, fire— may damage your assets. Improper use or poor maintenance may damage equipment. Inventory might be damaged in shipping or by pests.

K Risks of burglary, robbery, theft, or vandalism: Someone may break into your store during the night, damaging property and stealing inventory. Shoplifting costs many businesses significant losses. Vandals may spray paint on your building or break your windows.

K Risks to the ability of your business to perform adequately: A poor economy might stifle your market. Increased material costs might hinder your ability to be competitive. The illness or death of a key person might disrupt important functions of the company.

K Risks of penalties or litigation: You may be fined for violations of safety, environmental, tax, and other laws and regulations. You may be sued for sexual harassment, discrimination, or wrongful dismissal.

There's nothing you can do that will completely neutralize every risk, but an effective risk management program can reduce to an acceptable level the chances of something happening that will jeopardize the well-being of your business, your employees, or yourself. There are four elements to a risk management program:

K Eliminating risk
K Reducing risk
K Transferring risk
K Accepting risk

Eliminating Risk

While on a morning airline flight a few years ago, I asked the flight attendant for a glass of milk with my breakfast. "I'm afraid we don't have milk," she apologized.

"You've run out?" I asked.

"No," she explained. "We've recently stopped serving milk because we had trouble keeping it from spoiling while sitting in our service carts."

The airline had recognized that serving milk on a flight involved a health risk to passengers. They apparently determined that the benefit of including milk in their service was not worth the risk. So they eliminated it. No milk; no risk.

I've noticed in recent years that many companies have discontinued certain services to eliminate risks. I needed a couple of pieces of lumber to fix my fence recently. I asked the salesperson at the home store if they would cut my boards to length for me. "Our insurance company made us get rid of our saw for safety reasons," she told me. In other words, they eliminated the risk of an accident occurring with the saw. When I pulled my car to the back of the store to pick up my lumber, I asked the service person if he had something to tie down the uncut boards that would extend out my trunk. He offered me some twine but explained, "I can help you load the materials, but I'm not allowed to tie anything myself." This policy protected the company from any liability that might occur if the customer lost part of the load while in traffic. It eliminated a risk.

Discontinuing a product or service to eliminate a risk is a legitimate business decision if the risk and potential liability are clearly greater than the value that the product or service brings to your company. Be sure to recognize, though, that the real value of a product or service may exceed the revenues directly generated by it. If your customers are used to you providing a particular product or service, or if it is a product or service that a business like yours is expected to provide, discontinuing it could cost you customers. I probably won't go back to the home store that wouldn't cut my lumber, especially if I can find one that will. It isn't a matter of my being upset with them or not understanding their predicament. I just want to find the store that can best take care of my needs.

Reducing Risk

Many of the risks you encounter will be inherent to running a business. You won't be able to completely eliminate these without undermining your business, but there are usually ways to reduce risk. Methods of reducing risk fall into two general categories:

K Reducing the liability associated with the risk
K Reducing the chance of the problem occurring

In chapter 14 I told the story of Dave who lost $10,000 worth of paint when it froze in his warehouse. The following year, Dave reduced his risk by reducing the liability associated with the risk. He kept only $1000 in paint in the warehouse at a time. He could also have reduced the chance of the problem occurring by adding more insulation to the warehouse. When convenience stores keep only $50 in the cash register at a time, they reduce the liability associated with a robbery. By advertising this fact, they presumably reduce the chance of a robbery occurring. Most of your opportunities to reduce risk will primarily involve reducing the chance of a problem occurring, but don't neglect to look for opportunities to limit liability as well.

The best all-purpose way to reduce risk is through training. This often means developing effective systems and teaching your employees to use them properly. Sometimes, though, it simply means gathering accurate information and communicating it to your employees. Let's look at one actual situation and four hypothetical situations involving specific risks from each of the five categories I identified earlier in this chapter and see how practical training reduces the risks.

When I owned Sylvan, we had a furniture manufacturing facility. We built study stations, bookcases, and tables used by our students. Roger managed our shop, which employed two craftsmen besides himself. He recognized that, although he and his employees were experienced wood workers, the regular use of table saws, joiners, routers, and other power tools presented a safety risk. They all knew the basic safety rules but often got in a hurry and ignored them. So Roger developed a system. The system involved a series of safety steps that must be completed before operating any equipment.

1. Are you wearing goggles or protective glasses?
2. Are you wearing hearing protection?
3. Are the proper guards correctly installed on the equipment?
4. Is there anything blocking the motor or the blade?

Roger insisted that his employees learn the four steps, but getting them to follow them was another matter. So he came up with an idea to motivate his employees to implement the training. At the beginning of every month, Roger put $50 into an envelope. Every time he caught one of his employees violating the safety system, he took $10 out. At the end of the month the two employees split the remaining money. It's not a lot, but it worked. Roger rarely observed a safety violation and we never had a serious accident. The proper system and the right training technique reduced our safety risks.

Kay is a florist who owns her own company. The company owns a van, which it uses for deliveries. A few months ago the van started running roughly, so Kay had one of the drivers take it to a service center. The problem wasn't serious, but the mechanic explained to Kay that, if she didn't start a regular maintenance program on the vehicle, she would likely have a serious problem soon. Together they worked out a schedule based on mileage. Kay then developed a system whereby after each delivery the driver records the mileage of the van on the company's copy of the sales receipt. The bookkeeper then transfers the mileage from the receipt to a chart that is kept next to the maintenance schedule, regularly comparing the two and making maintenance appointments when necessary. Once Kay had trained her drivers and her bookkeeper with the system, her maintenance concerns were alleviated, and she had reduced the risk of damage to the van.

Amy's electronics repair shop was broken into a few months ago. The thieves took televisions, VCRs, and stereos belonging to her customers. What really frustrated Amy, though, was that she had difficulty getting her insurance company to pay the claim because *her security system hadn't been turned on.* Two of Amy's employees had closed the store the evening before, and both said they thought the other had taken care of it.

The day after the burglary, Amy developed a system for closing the store, a series of steps that must be performed in order each evening. It began with checking the bathrooms and the lunchroom to make sure no one was hiding there and ended with turning on the security system and locking the front door. Every employee who might be given the responsibility of closing the store was required to learn the system and complete it in Amy's presence before being left to do it alone. And, as part of the work schedule, Amy identified a particular employee each day to be responsible for closing. Once the employees were trained on this system, the security system was never forgotten again, and Amy reduced her risk of burglary.

Gavin has long been aware of how valuable Sandy is to his lawn care business. She not only performs all the in-house accounting functions, she also takes all the job orders and schedules all the company's work, coordinating the season-long contracts with the one-time jobs. Every morning when Gavin's employees arrive for work, Sandy has their assignments ready.

Lately Gavin has been concerned with what might happen to his business if something were to happen to Sandy. What if she becomes ill, decides to go back to school, or leaves the company for any reason? First Gavin asked Sandy to help him develop a job description for her position. Together they identified all the tasks Sandy performed and documented the systems Sandy used for each. Gavin hopes Sandy never leaves, but he's become much more comfortable knowing that, if she does leave, he now has the material to train someone to fill her position. He has reduced the risk of a change in personnel seriously affecting the ability of his business to serve its customers.

James is a roofing contractor. A recent job of his was inspected, and he was fined because, among other things, none of his employees wore safety harnesses with secured ropes while on the roof. James hadn't known what the regulations were and hadn't ever bothered to find out. The next day, he called the Occupational Safety and Health Administration (OSHA) and soon received the information he needed. He used it to educate himself and train his employees. By doing so, he reduced his risk not only of injury, but of fines and lawsuits as well.

Transferring Risk

Transferring risk usually means buying insurance. The risk still exists, but the insurance company has, for a price, assumed it for you. You can buy insurance for virtually every risk you can possibly think of. Here is a list of a few common types; a competent insurance agent can explain each of these and others:

- Fire insurance
- Liability insurance
- Automobile insurance
- Business interruption insurance
- Crime insurance
- Key personnel insurance

Strategies of reducing risk and transferring risk work well together. In the same way that a good driving record will reduce your automobile insurance premiums, many risk reduction plans can save you money on other insurance. Safety equipment and classes, as well as sexual harassment awareness training, may reduce liability insurance premiums. And security and sprinkler systems will likely reduce crime and fire insurance premiums. Talk to your insurance agent about what kind of discounts your business might be able to earn through risk reduction programs.

Accepting Risk

We all accept a certain amount of risk every day. We don't have any choice. There may be certain risks you choose to accept as a business owner, too. What is usually meant by accepting risk is self-insurance. In other words, you might create your own contingency fund to pay for unforeseen losses. If you choose to manage some of your risks this way, though, be careful not to underestimate potential liabilities.

The best system of risk management for your business will probably be some combination of eliminating risk, reducing risk, transferring risk, and accepting risk. You may not be able to prevent every mishap, but you can certainly be prepared for most contingencies. Just remember that no matter what happens, your business is ninety percent what you make it.

K   K   K   K

Before developing a risk management program, Denise decided to identify risks faced by Pilanimals, Inc. that should be of concern. Here's what she came up with:

- K Fire or some other disaster damaging inventory or equipment
- K Crime including burglary and vandalism
- K Civil liability such as for an accident
- K Fines for violating government regulations
- K Just not selling enough Pilanimals to pay the bills

In her risk management program, Denise incorporated elements of reducing, transferring, and accepting risk. Here's what she came up with:

Reducing Risk

Denise had smoke detectors and fire extinguishers installed, reducing the risk of damage by fire. She also had all the locks re-keyed to make sure no former tenant had access, reducing the risk of burglary. Greg, it turned out, was a volunteer emergency medical technician, which in itself reduced the risk of an accident resulting in more serious consequences than necessary. Denise enlisted Greg's help in assembling and maintaining a first aid kit, further reducing this risk. Finally, she made several phone calls to make sure they were aware of and in compliance with all applicable regulations, reducing their risk of fines.

Transferring Risk

Denise purchased two insurance policies for Pilanimals, Inc. besides worker's compensation, which wasn't optional. The first and most expensive was a liability plan. The second was a comprehensive property protection plan, but since they had less than $10,000 worth of assets to insure, this policy was reasonably inexpensive.

Accepting Risk

The last risk on her list, that they would make enough sales to stay in business, was one they would accept. It was a risk every entrepreneur took. Then again, almost everything they did as a company was designed to reduce that risk.

Denise looked into burglar and fire alarms and sprinkler systems, but the costs were too expensive for the value of their assets. Beyond the fire extinguishers and new locks, Denise and Duncan decided to accept the risk of burglary and fire.

With this risk management program, Duncan and Denise felt reasonably comfortable that no unforeseen circumstances would derail their vision for Pilanimals, Inc.

Establish Systems For External Operations

Chapter Seventeen

Defining Your Market and Targeting Your Customer

At some point in the planning of your business, you're likely to have *the dream*. The nightmare, actually. The one where you wake up in a cold sweat having dreamt that you opened your doors for business and nobody came. No customers. None. There you were with your systems in place, your staff hired and trained, your financial record-keeping system set up, everything clean and shiny and inviting, but no customers. Well, shake off that terrifying image! The next few chapters will help to assure that will never happen to you.

No doubt about it, the rubber meets the road where the customer's dollar changes hands. How do you reach customers, persuade them to do business with you, and retain their patronage through repeat business? That is the question you will answer by developing your marketing plan.

The elements you will need to consider in building your plan include defining your market, identifying your target customer, positioning your product or service, pricing, promotion, and distribution.

137

Market Research

It is important at the outset of your planning to identify your market opportunity and gauge the outlook for that market. Doing so will involve what is called market research. Don't panic, now, it's a lot more fun than a college term paper!

Market research draws information from primary sources, secondary sources, or both. Collecting primary data entails gathering information that has not previously been compiled. For example, if you were to design a questionnaire that you sent out to prospective customers with a return envelope, the information you got back would be primary data. Recently, one of my colleagues, Paul, conducted an informal survey at a business expo. As business owners came by his booth, Paul asked them to complete the survey shown here.

What is your biggest challenge as a business owner? Check all that apply:

☐ Not enough time
☐ Not enough money
☐ Slow sales
☐ Can't find reliable employees
☐ Finding and keeping customers
☐ Ineffective advertising
☐ Clearly knowing what your business future is
☐ Bookkeeping and using your financial statements
☐ Other (please specify) _____

The results of this survey provided input potentially valuable in planning future services for business owners or developing promotion of existing services. The most frequently given answer, by the way, was "not enough time."

Similar surveys or questionnaires can be done by mail or phone, although you should know that mail response is likely to be low, so you will need to mail out a relatively large quantity in order to get a meaningful response. Expect a 5 to 10% return. As Paul did, keep the questions short, to the point, and easy to understand and answer. Direct the questionnaires to people who are most likely to be interested in your product or service. If mailing, enclose a cover letter explaining why the information is needed and thanking the respondent for their participation. A follow-up mailing can improve response rate.

Other forms of primary market research include interviews, group discussions, group surveys, and trials. Say, for example, you were to place your product in three selected locations at point-of-purchase displays marked at three different prices. The results after a week or two would tell you a lot about the marketability of the product and the appropriate pricing level. As you can imagine, market research is not as conclusive as scientific research because it is impossible to control all the variables. At best, it gives you some feedback from potential customers to guide you in making your marketing decisions.

Secondary market research involves using data that is already compiled. This kind of research is extremely cost-effective and useful for a small business. The best place to start is your local public library reference section. Librarians there are trained to assist you in finding the most beneficial reference materials for your purpose. Many useful reports are generated by the federal government. A few you should take a look at include:

Statistical Abstract of the United States

Issued annually, this report contains a statistical summary of economic factors.

Survey of Current Business

This is a monthly publication offering updated information on business statistics including sales and inventory levels as well as general economic trends.

State and Metropolitan Area Data Book

Issued by the Census Bureau, this report provides statistics specific to metropolitan areas, cities, and counties.

Case Studies in Using Data for Better Business Decisions

This publication gives income and age demographics by region.

US Industrial Outlook

This report provides statistics and five-year growth projections for 200 industries.

In addition to government-generated reports, there are a plethora of potentially pertinent publications including trade directories, business journals, and various business indices with which your librarian can acquaint you. Most public libraries now offer a computerized search of periodicals. While sitting at a computer terminal you can enter the subject you wish to read about, and the computer will scan the business periodicals and show you what has been published about that subject in reverse chronological order, most recent first. This system allows you to check in from time to time and efficiently get updated on your areas of interest.

I also recommend that you check with the Small Business Administration, who can offer a number of publications and can direct you to good sources of research material. They can also refer you to free or low-cost consultants who can guide you in your research efforts.

Defining Your Market

Before you begin your research, think carefully about what your market is. Janis, a friend of mine had always dreamed of having riding stables, offering boarding and care of horses and riding lessons. In doing her market research, she checked out the other riding stables, their prices and practices, cleanliness, visual appeal, etc. Janis decided she wanted to have the most appealing stables in the business. After a great deal of repair, rebuilding, painting, and the like, she opened her doors and started advertising to riding clubs and other groups involving horses. It was several months before she realized that the primary users of stables such as hers were teenage girls who viewed riding as a leisure activity interchangeable with any number of other after-school events. My friend then shifted her marketing focus to teens, emphasizing the entertainment value of horse riding as opposed to the cleanliness and upkeep of the stables. Her business increased.

It is important to define your market accurately. It is equally important to identify what other markets may overlap. In the case of the stables there was overlapping competition for the teenage girls' leisure dollar in movies, CDs, skateboarding, and "hangin' at the mall." Shifts in trends, fads, or demographics could effect the stables business.

Part of defining your market will entail identifying your competitors and learning as much about them as possible. Some of the questions you will want to answer about competitors will pertain to:

K policies: returns, exchanges, credit, etc.
K hours of operation
K number of locations

K number of employees
K pricing
K guarantees
K delivery
K promotional strategy

Once you have gathered this information and achieved a familiarity with competitors in your field, you will be able to identify your key competitors and analyze their strengths and weaknesses. This will provide a basis for differentiating your business from theirs.

Targeting Your Customer

Targeting your customer is an ongoing process that will be greatly enhanced by the information you'll gain as your business develops and you have sales and customer histories to draw from. In the planning stage, common sense and intuition are likely to serve you nearly as well as sophisticated marketing research. For example, if you are selling a delivery service that delivers food from upscale restaurants to people's homes, chances are you will be targeting relatively affluent families. Knowing that, you can then consult statistical reports to identify zip codes where per-household incomes tend to be higher. Now you have a pretty good guess as to who your customers will be and where they live. Armed with this information you can select methods of reaching those customers with your selling message. You might try direct mail, telemarketing, or driving your classy-looking delivery van (clearly displaying your business name and number) through their neighborhoods. At some point you will begin to get sales. When you do, you can glean information from your customers to learn more about them and customize your marketing and services to better fit their needs.

Using the old newspaper reporter's trick involving the 5 W's and H (who, what, where, when, why, and how), you can shape a basic customer-targeting analysis. *Who* are your potential customers? *What* can you offer them that they are not getting now? *Where* are your potential customers located? *Why* should they do business with you? *When* are the peak seasons or times to reach these customers? *How* many of them are there? The answers to these questions will provide direction for your promotional strategies so that you can accurately and efficiently get the right message to the right people.

Once you have done your market research using primary and secondary sources, defined your target market, and identified your target customer, you will be ready to consider the issues of positioning and pricing your product or service. All of these factors will be key to shaping a powerful and consistent promotion strategy.

In the next chapter we'll discuss how price and positioning are closely related. We'll look at some pricing strategies and see how psychological factors can affect buying behaviors.

K   K   K   K

Duncan's primary research consisted of the development and field-testing of his first few Pilanimals in the radiology lab of the hospital where he worked. He knew from that experience that children were comforted by the Pilanimal and were more likely to be still, allowing for a successful x-ray. Fewer retakes were needed if a Pilanimal was used.

After construction of the first few Pilanimals, which were modeled after panda bears, Denise began experimenting with other colors and "species" such as the Dino-Pilanimal, which looked like a goofy, friendly dinosaur. Later, Duncan asked Denise to make a bright yellow chick, a lop-eared bunny, and a spotted, puppy Pilanimal. Duncan liked to let his patients choose the Pilanimal they liked best.

The Dino-Pilanimal was quite popular with all kids, and the bunny was a favorite among Duncan's younger patients. The puppy and the panda did all right, but for some reason the chick was rarely chosen. Duncan also found that some children requested animals that he didn't have. The most popular requests were ponies, monkeys, and, surprisingly, lions. Denise experimented with these suggestions with reasonable success except with the lion. There just wasn't an efficient way to represent the mane. So she elected to try a tiger, but the stripes posed production challenges. Finally she gave up on large cats and made a cuddly kitten, which turned out to be one of the more popular pilanimals. Eventually they settled on six different species. And each of these designs except the panda could be made in many different colors and with various combinations of features. The puppy, for instance, might have any number of large or small spots on its back or just one spot around one of its eyes. Denise had designed two sets of puppy ears to choose from—one floppy and one stand-up. Some puppies came with their tongues hanging out, some with big droopy eyes, and some with upturned noses. Incorporating a number of variations in each species made production much more interesting without really taking any longer and also created the impression that no two Pilanimals were alike, a feature that Duncan later found to be a useful sales tool.

Duncan's field-testing also showed him that x-ray technicians liked using Pilanimals. Most of them were very caring people whose hearts went out to the hurt and frightened children who required x-rays. These technicians were highly motivated to do anything they could to comfort and cheer these little patients.

Duncan and Denise did their secondary market research at the reference library, identifying population growth trends, geographic distribution of medical facilities, and contact information on hospitals, clinics, and health maintenance organizations.

Denise suggested that they initially target hospitals within a tri-state area. Denise's friend, Karla, was a sales representative for a medical supplies company and provided Denise with a database of hospitals in that area and names of the purchasing agents. Duncan obtained a list of names from his professional association so that he could match technicians' names to hospitals, Although the x-ray technicians would not be making the final purchasing decision, Duncan knew that it would be imperative to gain their enthusiastic support before presenting to the hospital administrators.

Having done their homework—both with primary and secondary market research—Duncan and Denise felt confident that they had properly identified their market and their target customer and that they were appropriately equipped to launch a successful marketing campaign and sell a lot of Pilanimals.

Chapter Eighteen

Strategy for the Pricing Wars

Pricing your product or service appropriately is absolutely essential to business success. Clearly, the price you are able to command must exceed your costs in order for you to survive. By the same token, the price must seem reasonable to the customer in exchange for the perceived value of what you are selling. Although this may seem pretty straightforward, you will see as we examine pricing issues that determining the optimum pricing strategy will require research, intuition, and astute observation.

Cost-plus is one way to start thinking about pricing requirements. After all, cost plus *something* is your bare minimum price. It is often joked that some businesses price to sell at a loss but make it up in volume. Clearly, a high-volume of sales makes it possible to sell at a lower mark-up from cost, but there must *always* be a mark-up. When calculating costs, it is important to take *all* costs into consideration. Your business will have fixed costs, like the lease on your place of business, and variable costs, like the cost of materials. The price of your goods or services must reflect a per-unit share of all these expenses plus a profit in order to make doing business worthwhile. Once that figure is established, a number of other factors should be taken into account including:

K strength of the market
K prices of your competitors
K demand for your product
K quality of your product
K seasonal influences
K positioning of your product

Bear in mind that, as any of these factors change, you will need to consider adjusting your prices.

Let's look at an example to illustrate some of these points. Suppose that you were operating a gift shop. It is September, and you are stocking in preparation for Christmas shoppers. An artisan comes into your shop hoping to sell some hand-crafted glass angels for $3.50 each. Confident that you can sell and make a reasonable profit on these angels, you purchase several dozen. How then shall you price them for retail sale? Clearly, you will need to sell them for more than $3.50 each in order to break even. You have expenses to cover that exceed the acquisition of the merchandise. The bulk of items you sell in your store must yield enough revenue to cover acquisition costs, overhead, and profit. You know that angels are a popular gift item and are particularly so during the Christmas holidays. You have seen a similar glass angel, but of lesser quality, selling at a competitive store for $8.99. The angels you have purchased are more aesthetically pleasing and appear to be of better quality. You decide to merchandise the angels in a display along with other, more expensive gift items and price them at $11.99. As the Christmas shopping season begins, the angels sell slowly at first, but pick up with the increasing volume of customers as the holiday approaches. A week before Christmas you decide to drop the price of the remaining angels to $9.99 in order to sell the balance before Christmas. After Christmas there are four angels remaining. You mark them down to $4.99 and sell them out.

In this hypothetical, you have considered the cost of the item ($3.50 plus your expenses), prices of your competitors ($8.99), demand for your product (angels are popular), quality of your product (superior to your competitor's), seasonal influences (demand increases until Christmas, then drops off), and positioning of the product (you elect to display it with higher-priced items, thereby associating it with greater value).

Some retailers determine mark-up by calculating their total operating expenses as a percentage of sales. This is done by using the net sales figure from their annual income statement and calculating the total operating expenses as a percentage of that figure. Then the retailer may choose a target profit percentage, say of 10% before taxes. If, for example, the operating expenses as a percentage of sales were 32%, the retailer would add 10% to 32% to ascertain a percent-of-sales figure that must be added to the acquisition cost of the item—in this case, 42%. To find the corresponding sales price, the cost is then divided by the complement of the markup as follows: 100% - 42% = 58%. $3.50 (the cost of the angel) divided by 58% = $6.03. By selling the angel at $6.00 you could have met your goal of 10% profit after costs. Because of the seasonal nature of the item and other factors discussed above, however, you were able to sell it for considerably more.

Positioning Your Product or Service

Your need to cover costs and make a profit are one part of the pricing equation. The other side involves the customer, the customer's needs, the customer's perception of the value of your product, and how the customer views your product relative to your competitors' products. Of course, not all customers see things the same way or engage in the same purchase-decision behaviors. Consider the following story.

One lovely summer evening, just after sunset, a young woman named Cynthia waited for her date to arrive. The warm, still, summer air carried the scent of lilac blooms and wisteria, hinting of the pleasures of the season. Within a few minutes Cynthia's date arrived, carrying a parcel. Excited, Cynthia looked forward to receiving a romantic gift. As the gift was presented, Cynthia opened the box to find 50 Hershey bars. Seeing that she was perplexed, Cynthia's date explained that he had intended to purchase a 2-pound box of Godiva chocolates for her but learned that the difference in the per-pound production costs between Godiva chocolates and Hershey bars was only a few cents, that the quality of the chocolate was nearly equal. So instead of investing his money in Godiva chocolate, where he would be paying a price for fancy packaging and advertising, he decided to invest the same amount of money in Hershey bars, thereby giving Cynthia a much better value. The following day Cynthia began looking for a new boyfriend. Where did Cynthia's suitor go wrong?

Perceived value and product positioning are at the heart of this ill-fated love story. For Cynthia, the expensive box of chocolates has value that goes far beyond the production costs. The beautiful packaging, the product promotion involving images of elegance, luxury, and romance, the status attached to the product name—all of these things add value to the product. The same dollar equivalent in drug store candy bars was no equivalent at all! The candy bars suggested no romance, no refinement, no mystique. For Cynthia's date to surmise that the difference in pricing was simply a result of packaging and advertising was accurate but short-sighted. In some situations, packaging and image are worth their weight in gold!

As you evaluate your business for the purpose of developing a marketing plan, you will want to consider how to position your products or services relative to the market. Will you provide a high-end, exclusive product or service emphasizing superior quality and status? Will you shoot for the middle of the market and emphasize reliability or value for the dollar? Will you go for the lower end and appeal to economy-minded customers? Your business's or product's position in the market should be sufficiently defined that you can articulate it, include it in your marketing plan, and maintain consistency in your position throughout your marketing efforts.

Clearly, price and position are interrelated. A well-known cosmetics company whose products are sold exclusively in department stores once decided to introduce a mascara priced affordably to demonstrate their desire to deliver value to the customer. They priced the product at $5.00, which was a fraction of what competitors were charging for similar items and a fraction of what they, themselves, had charged in the past for mascaras. Much to their astonishment, the line did not sell well at all. The price was so far below what shoppers considered customary that the quality of the product was called into question and shoppers hesitated to buy. Seeing that they had misjudged their strategy, the cosmetics company recalled all the product, put it in different packaging, repriced it at $19.95 and redistributed it to department stores. This time, the mascara sold well and generated repeat sales to happy customers. The moral of the story: once you have established your niche, it can be perilous to deviate from it, even by offering customers a bargain!

The numerous psychological issues that go into positioning and pricing are fodder for an enormous amount of research and subsequent literature. Libraries and periodicals are full of it, and much of it is fascinating reading. Take for example the practice of pricing everything with a "9" on the end, as in $5.99, $999.00, or 39 cents. Does this really cause consumers to buy more, somehow feeling that $5.99 is significantly less than $6.00? Apparently, a lot of retailers think so, despite the fact that research has been inconclusive. Some consumers will assume that a higher price necessarily means better quality and will consequently purchase the more expensive of two items when no other difference is perceived. You've probably heard that, in supermarkets, people are more likely to purchase merchandise displayed at eye level than merchandise on lower or higher shelves. The psychology of consumer behavior is as varied and fascinating as people themselves.

Then there's the question of what you sell versus what customers buy. You may sell shoes, for example, but customers are likely to be buying fashion, comfort, status, an image of athleticism, or personal indulgence. You may be selling Mercedes automobiles—well-built, quality cars. But, trust me, your customers aren't buying reliable transportation as much as they're buying status, luxury, and an emblem of success. Almost always, a customer is hoping to receive benefits from a purchase that exceed the technical description of the product or service. Customers may hope to get convenience, for example, or comfort, or safety, or beauty, or status, or fun. Maybe they're looking for security, or health, or youth, or peace of mind. The customer has needs for these intangibles, needs that you can speak to once you have identified them and associated them with what you're selling. The better you know your customers and prospective customers, the more you will understand their needs and buying behaviors, and the better you will be able to match your marketing message, packaging, and pricing to their preferences.

K K K K

Duncan and Denise sat at Duncan's kitchen table sipping lemonade. "What do you think a hospital would pay for a Pilanimal?" Denise asked.

"I don't know," Duncan responded. "I know that a Pilanimal saves the hospital money. X-ray retakes are expensive, and the insurance companies don't pay for retakes. Using a Pilanimal really helps to quiet the patient and get a good shot the first time. That's worth something."

"And if the hospital lets the child keep the Pilanimal and take it home," Denise added, "the result is a happier patient and grateful parents. There is clearly some public relations value in that for the hospital."

"Would it be difficult to put the hospital's name on the Pilanimal?"

"Not at all," Denise said. "Our sewing machines have letter-embroidery features."

"That would enhance the PR value of the Pilanimals to the hospital or clinic. And we could probably charge more for that."

Duncan and Denise calculated all their expenses and costs. That actual cost of production materials was about $5.90 per unit. This did not include labor and other expenses, but just the cost of the nylon, thread, and polyester fiberfill. Then they considered some other factors that might affect their pricing:

Strength of the Market

Duncan knew that the changes in health care included a focus on cost savings as well as a shift toward health maintenance organizations and growing competition among health-care providers. Because Pilanimals could clearly save money for hospitals and clinics, there would be a strong market for them. The PR value would help health-care providers market their services and strengthen their image in the community.

Prices of Competitors

There currently were no competitors in this market.

Demand for the Product

Duncan knew he would have to create the demand for Pilanimals through promotion, but he trusted the reception would be positive and subsequent demand would be high. Based on his market research, he knew that an average community hospital did a minimum of ten pediatric x-rays per day. If a Pilanimal was used for each one, that would be roughly 300 Pilanimals per hospital per month.

Quality of the Product

Denise and Duncan were committed to providing a consistently high-quality product that would be appealing and would hold up well as a toy after being taken home from the hospital by the child.

Seasonal Influences

Although the number of pediatric x-rays increased somewhat during the summer months as children engaged in more outdoor play, the seasonal variation was not enough to warrant pricing changes.

Positioning of the Product

Duncan knew that positioning the product as a cost-savings tool would be enough to sell Pilanimals. Pushing the PR value to the hospitals and clinics would further add value. These two factors would be central in the positioning of Pilanimals.

Duncan and Denise used the calculations of their expenses and their production costs to see what they would need to produce and sell to make a profit. Then they considered the market factors listed above and decided to price the Pilanimals at $26 each with an additional $2 per unit charge for putting the hospital name on the Pilanimal's tummy.

Chapter Nineteen

Promotion: Have I Got a Deal for You!

Promotion can be one of the most exciting and creative areas of endeavor in running your business. It is an area where it is not only possible, but necessary, to define the character and personality of your business and convey it in powerful ways to current and prospective customers. Promotion means engaging in communications that will persuade people to do business with you. Promotional activities such as advertising and public relations will help to attract new customers, to build loyalty among existing customers, to solidify an image in the public eye, to support the efforts of your sales people, and to differentiate you from your competition. In this chapter we'll be discussing some ways to do promotion on a budget and to make every promotional dollar count.

Advertising is expensive. Done right, it's powerful and worth every penny. Done poorly, it can be money down the proverbial hole. Shot-gun advertising that is poorly-focused and unclear in its message costs just as much to run as well-targeted, effective advertising. It is imperative to develop a well-thought-out promotional plan utilizing the right message, the right media, and the right frequency. With carefully targeted customers being reached with the right message, your promotional dollars can provide satisfying results.

There are many different estimates of the optimal number of times to run an ad. No one knows for sure, but studies seem to indicate that a prospective customer is likely to notice your ad only one out of three times he is exposed to it. Further, studies suggest that the prospective customer must notice the ad eight to ten times before the message really sinks in. You can see, if you accept these estimates, you will need to run an ad three multiplied by eight to ten times, or a total of 24 to 30 times in order for your message to be fully realized. Of course, the better the ad copy, the better the results. And, for this reason, is will probably be worthwhile to have a professional design the ad.

Trying to save a little money up front by foregoing professional help is often a false economy. If it costs $400 to run an ad and you run it 30 times, that will cost you $12,000. Unless you have training and talent in advertising design, your options may be as follows:

	Design Cost	Ad Cost	Total	Results
Do-it-yourself	$0	$12,000	$12,000	Poor
Professional	$600	$12,000	$12,600	Great

I don't mean to imply that you are necessarily lacking in skill or creativity. It's possible that you could design an ad that would perform just as well as anything an agency could come up with. But it's been my observation that most people underestimate what's involved in designing a good ad. Like so many things, it looks so simple when it's done really well that we tend to underestimate the talent and judgment involved. Professional advertising people are not only creative—they know the rules. And, if they're really good, they know when to break the rules. These are the kinds of judgment calls that most of us are not trained to make.

Of course, if your target customers are in an area where media access is inexpensive, you may have more leeway for experimentation without busting your budget. There's nothing wrong with doing a little ad copy yourself and trying it to see what happens, *if* you can afford it.

Speaking of spending money on advertising, just how do you go about setting an advertising budget? If you are just starting a business, this will be more challenging. Established businesses use one of a variety of methods, the most common being the percentage-of-sales approach. Of course, you need a sales history to do this. The calculation is done as follows:

$$\textit{Advertising-to-Sales Ratio} = \frac{\textit{Advertising Expenses for the Year}}{\textit{Sales for the Year}} \times 100$$

If, for example, your business had sales of \$220,000 and had spent \$12,000 on advertising that year, you would divide \$12,000 by \$220,000 getting .054. Then you would multiply .054 by 100 getting 5.4%. You would allocate 5.4% of your projected sales for the next year for advertising.

Obviously, if you are just starting, you don't have a sales history from which to calculate. In that event, I would recommend contacting your trade association for information on the typical advertising-to-sales ratio for your type of business. Take that percentage times your first-year projected sales. Then, because you are a new business and will have to invest more in advertising to get the customer's attention, double or triple that number. As you plan your monthly advertising expenditures, consider what seasonal factors may influence your business, when you might be introducing new products or services, or when you might be pushing into new geographical areas for sales. Clearly, some months will require heavier advertising expenditures than others.

Media

Once you decide how much you can spend on advertising, you will need to consider what kind of advertising to purchase. For example, if your business calls for mass-media advertising, you will be considering print advertising, broadcast advertising, and direct mail. The work you have done identifying your customer will help you tremendously in selecting the best media to use for advertising. You know where your customers or prospective customers are located geographically. You have studied their demographics, so you know their average income range, their age range, the average size of their families, and the kinds of occupations they choose. From this information you can deduce some of the more promising placements for advertising that will get your message to these customers.

Print advertising includes newspapers and magazines. Newspapers garner the highest percentage of advertising dollars annually with television running a close second. There are, of course, differences in circulation of magazines and newspapers ranging from local and regional publications to national publications. Within a city you will usually find one or more community newspapers that strive to serve the entire metropolitan area as well as smaller, specialty newspapers catering to the interests of a specific group. If that group is one you are targeting, ads in that specialty paper will be a bargain for you. Advertising rates will vary depending upon a number of factors, the most important being circulation. If you contact the sales office of any of these publications and request a "media kit," they will send you statistics about their circulation, geographical reach, readership, ad rates, and perhaps other useful information. Although ad rates are negotiable, the media kit will give you an idea of the expense relative to the cost of advertising in other publications. Magazines, too, vary in size, distribution, and geographical reach. Consider whether your targeted customer is likely to read the publication. If the answer is yes, then go on to consider other factors such as cost.

Print media charge for advertising by column-inches. An ad might be two columns wide, for example, and two inches tall. This would constitute four column-inches.

Broadcast media, as you would guess, include radio and television, both network and cable. The proliferation of cable television service has created many new advertising opportunities, some of them quite affordable when cabled to a localized area. If you have seen some of the cable shopping channels, you have witnessed a new phenomenon in advertising. It is amazing to think that people would purposely tune in to watch advertising, but they do. These shopping programs attract shoppers by the hundreds of thousands and sell in quantities that make it possible to discount the prices sharply from other retailers. It blends the advantages of a mail-order catalogue with personal selling, a powerful combination. As you would image, it can be expensive to have your goods featured on a national cable shopping show, but most local cable markets also have video classifieds and other less-expensive advertising opportunities.

The cost of broadcast advertising varies tremendously depending on the reach, the viewership (or number of listeners), the time slot (also called the daypart), and the positioning relative to other programming. For television, the most expensive time slot tends to be in the evening from 7:30 to 10:00. Radio's prime time is in the morning from 6:00 to 10:00. This is known as "drive time" because people listen to radio as they drive their cars to work. People who never listen to radio any other time will often listen during drive time.

Television advertising tends to cost about 10 times what you would pay for equivalent radio advertising. Part of this is production costs, and part is because of the cost of air time. Television has the advantage of engaging another sense, thereby creating what may be a more memorable message. At one time television also claimed to have a less fragmented audience than radio. Because radio has always had a significant number of stations serving each area, it was argued that you could capture a larger share of the audience by advertising on television, which was focused in three major networks. With the advent of cable television, however, the television audience has become increasingly fragmented. Bruce Springsteens's song, "Fifty-seven Channels and Nothin' On," comes to mind. Add to that scenario the effect of the remote control "channel surfing" and the challenge of capturing a viewer's attention becomes clear.

Still, television advertising works. Otherwise, you wouldn't see so much of it. In attempting to meet the challenge of reaching viewers without going broke, advertisers are experimenting with a number of methods including the use of very short spots (often repeated within the same commercial break) to get more exposures. Some have developed co-marketing ads that manage to convey positive messages about more than one product in the same spot. Take, for example, an ad suggesting that a high-quality, sexy automobile like Model Q should be polished with a high-quality wax like Brand R. Then show the proud owner admiring his newly-waxed car while enjoying Beverage E with a beautiful woman on his arm. Three products, one spot.

Because television advertising engages the sense of sight as well as hearing, people are more likely to remember it. The use of movement and color further enhance memorability. Advertising on television enhances a company's public image and tends to get a quicker response than other media. Overall, television is a great way to advertise, but because it is expensive, you will want to carefully consider alternatives before investing too much of your budget in television.

Direct mail allows you tremendous selectivity in your advertising audience. Say, for example, you were selling a line of sporty, upscale automobile accessories. You could get a mailing list of everyone within a specified geographic area who had purchased a sports car within the last five years. If you did not want to purchase that entire list, you could ask to purchase the addresses on that list ending in an odd number. This would give you half of the list, spread over the same geographical area. You could do a test run with those addresses, then, based on the response, decide if you wanted to purchase the other half of the list. The point is, mailing lists can be selected with great detail, giving you great targeting power.

A good rule of thumb for direct mail is that a minimum of four mailings to the same customer is required to get a response. You will probably be wasting your resources if you plan fewer than four mailings. As a consumer, you have received direct mail advertising. When you get home from work in the evening, you probably park your car, take your mail from the mail box, glance at it as you walk to the front door of your home, walk inside, and throw away about half of your mail having identified it as "junk mail." You may not even have looked at it except to see that it was advertising. This is why repeat mailings are necessary.

Some advertisers believe post cards are a good way to go for direct mail. The materials and postage costs are less and the consumer is likely to see your message on the card, even as they throw it away. Others argue that direct mail should always be a letter so that it is not so easily identified as advertising right away and you have an opportunity to catch the reader's interest and communicate a full sales message.

Direct mail tends to cost more per reader than other avenues of advertising, but clearly has the advantage of allowing you to focus more tightly on your target audience.

Internet Advertising

More and more businesses are posting advertising and public relations materials for access by internet users. The internet can be a very inexpensive way to reach a large number of people all over the world. You can literally be doing business internationally overnight. All of the hype and hubbub about the internet is being generated by the potential that it holds for doing business. That potential is a long way from being fully realized at this point, but many businesses don't want to miss out on the development toward an easily accessible global marketplace. Getting on the "net" is not something you necessarily need to do during the busy early stages of starting your business, but at some point you will want to explore the possibilities.

Yellow Pages

As a new business, you *need* to be listed in the yellow pages. Surveys show that when consumers use the yellow pages, they have a specific purchase in mind and are looking for providers of that product or service. They will use the yellow pages to find the phone numbers of those providers, then call the providers directly to learn more. Their purchasing choices depend on what they learn from the providers, not what they read in the ads. This would suggest that you do not necessarily have to run a large or multi-color ad in order to benefit greatly from a yellow pages listing, but being listed is imperative.

Billboards, Busses, Bus Benches, Ball Parks

There are, of course, lots of places to put advertising. Outdoor advertising in high-traffic areas results in many people seeing your ad. Those people who travel along that route often will have multiple exposures to the ad. Because people are usually in transit when they see these ads, the message must be brief and powerful. Costs vary depending on the size of the community and the desirability of the location.

As a new business owner you will find that advertising salespeople seek you out. They may be very aggressive and make claims for their advertising that sound fabulous. Be sure that you investigate and compare many avenues before committing your precious advertising dollars. Also be sure that your advertising is in line with your mission statement and with the image and positioning that you have elected for your business. Check for clarity and impact of the message, then track carefully to assess the results of your advertising. One easy way to do this is simply to ask new customers where they heard about you and make a note on their customer profile card. This will give you data that can then be compiled to learn about the impact and cost-effectiveness of your advertising.

K   K   K   K

Duncan came back to the office to find Denise singing:

Pilanimals, Pilanimals,
They look like funny animals!
I'd love to cuddle up to one,
They make my x-rays lots more fun.

"You're getting punchy, Denise," Duncan said.

"We're going to have to find some way to promote these things," Denise responded.

"Thankfully we won't need to run mass-market commercials," Duncan said.

After work that evening, Duncan and Denise stopped by a coffee shop and sketched out a promotional plan. Here are some of the possibilities they identified:

- direct mail
- trade shows
- personal selling
- telemarketing
- partnering with a medical supplies company
- developing a video
- printing brochures
- advertising in a mail-order catalogue

Recognizing that many of these options involved prohibitive expense, they decided on the following plan.

They would hire a photographer to take color pictures of several different Pilanimals. Then they would assemble these pictures in an 8 x 11 inch montage, representing each of the six species of Pilanimals in different colors and with different features. Duncan would compose a letter including a sales message and ordering information. The letter would be sent to the radiology department of major hospitals along with a free Pilanimal. Duncan would then follow up with telephone calls to establish rapport with prospective customers, get feedback from them, and take orders.

Chapter Twenty

Put Your Best Foot Forward: Public Relations

The term "public relations" refers to the overall impression of your company that gets communicated to the public. In a general sense, virtually anything you do has this potential. An act of goodwill toward a single person has public relations value as does a major feature story on television or in the press. Sponsoring a local Little League team or offering scholarships to distinguished graduating seniors at a local high school are both examples of communicating a positive message about your business to the public.

Often, public relations involves attracting the attention of the press and broadcast media. Getting news coverage is a powerful thing. It creates the impression that something exciting is happening. You've heard the expression that nothing succeeds like success. This is illustrated clearly by how the media's attention to your business draws people to your business. You're doing the same thing today that you did yesterday, but this morning your business was featured on the local television news. Suddenly the phones are ringing, new customers are coming in, other successful businesses are interested in doing business with you. It's been said that inch-for-inch, positive news coverage of your business is much more powerful than paid advertising. This is absolutely true.

A friend of mind, Tina-Louise, was operating a home-based business with her husband, Spike. They had a mail-order compact disc business called CD's We Bee. Being a bright and creative couple, Spike and Tina had developed a clever logo for their business featuring a bumble bee and had promoted their business at a number of community activities, once with Tina-Louise appearing in a bee costume to distribute coupons. They had a good stream of business going. When they reached a state of readiness to grow the business, Tina-Louise decided to apply her energies to public relations. She checked out a book from the public library that explained the basics of a press release. From those instructions, she constructed a press release about CD's We Bee and distributed it to the local newspaper and broadcast media. Within days the newspaper contacted them requesting more information and wanting to send out a photographer. The beautiful news story featuring this interesting local business ran on Sunday, the issue of the paper that gets the highest readership. Although Tina-Louise and Spike expected to get some new customers from this publicity, they were not prepared for the huge influx of phone calls and orders. In retrospect, Tina-Louise says that she should have arranged for temporary help to handle the high volume of calls generated by the publicity. She and Spike were not able to take all the calls that came in during the first few days after the article. They wish they had been better prepared to capitalize on the opportunity that good press generated. Still, CD's We Bee flourished in the aftermath of Tina-Louise's PR efforts and remains a strong business to this day.

One great way to get positive publicity is to become an "expert" in your field and make yourself available for public speaking engagements and interviews. Darrin, an energetic young man with a chimney-sweep and masonry-repair business, commented to me that his business tended to pick up whenever the local television news would do a public interest story on home safety that mentioned the need for chimney inspection and repair. Generally, this would happen in the fall when people first began using their fireplaces.

"Darrin," I asked him, "do you consider yourself an expert in chimney inspection, safety, and repair?"

"Of course," he said, "I'd better be!"

"Then, why don't you contact the local stations and offer your availability for interviews or sound bites? That would help to lend credibility and interest to their stories, and it might lead to more business for you."

Darrin took my suggestion. He was featured on a local telecast, which resulted in many new inquiries. Darrin parlayed that into new customers, customers whom he was able to service repeatedly to meet their chimney-inspection and masonry-repair needs. It cost him nothing but paid off big.

Remember that news media are "news hungry" a good deal of the time. Now that 24-hour news networks are flourishing both nationally and regionally, there is a greater-than-ever demand for interesting bits of information to put on the air. Contact some of those reporters with an interesting story and you'll be well-received.

If you have good writing skills, you might consider writing an article or a regular column for your community newspaper or for one of the trade or business journals that your customers read. This, too, establishes you as someone who is recognized as an expert. It builds your credibility and makes you known to greater numbers of people.

Sometimes combining a public relations effort with a promotional effort can work well. I once advertised an offer to donate a percentage of my proceeds to a local nonprofit organization that provided food and clothing for homeless children. It was my favorite charity because of the concrete nature of their activities, giving kids what they needed most in a very straightforward way. My aim was primarily to help kids, but the tie-in resulted in favorable publicity for my business as well.

If your business serves a localized area, you can probably do much of the public relations work yourself. It is advisable to pick up a book, as Tina-Louise did, on how to write a standard press release and use that format. Look for ways to be newsworthy. For example, if your business deals in products or services that are seasonal, put out a press release just before that season begins. This is what Darrin did with his chimney-sweep business. If your business involved weddings, you might want to put out a release in wedding fashion trends in the springtime, because a high percentage of weddings occur in the months of May and June. Look for ways to tie in to topics that the paper will probably be covering as a result of widespread interest.

If your business reach is national, you will want to engage the services of a public relations firm. Once you do, be sure that they produce for you. I once contracted with a PR firm at the advice of one of my employees who had seen this firm do excellent work for other businesses. After six months and an expenditure of $60,000, they had not generated one single piece of publicity for us. When I asked them about it, they told me that what I was doing just wasn't sufficiently newsworthy. I switched to a smaller firm who was much more enthusiastic about my business vision. Within three months they had scored three major hits in nationally distributed publications. I'm not saying that a smaller firm necessarily will do a better job than a larger one, but relatively speaking, I was a more important client to the smaller firm than I was to the bigger one. Consequently, I got better service and better results. Still, I think the main determinant was not so much the size as the spirit. If you interview a PR firm or an advertising agency and they seem to be giving you a ho-hum in response to your goals and vision for your company's future, pass them by. You'll have enough distracters in your life without having to pay for them! You deserve to have your professional marketing partners in your corner wholeheartedly!

K K K K

Duncan knew that Pilanimals had great human interest appeal, but he wanted most of the public relations value of Pilanimals to go to his customers. The first local hospital that placed a substantial standing order with the intent to give a Pilanimal to each pediatric x-ray patient was St. Patrick's Regional Medical Center. Duncan talked to Judy in the community relations department at St. Pat's to see if she might want to put out a press release to the local newspapers. Judy loved the idea and wrote up a press release about Duncan and Pilanimals, Inc. as well as St. Pat's decision to use the Pilanimals for the sake of their young patients. Judy took a picture of a four-year-old girl holding a Dino-Pilanimal while having her wrist x-rayed. She also took a picture of Duncan and wrote a summary of his background and how he got the idea for Pilanimals. All of this was sent to the local news media. Two newspapers carried the story and one television station sent a crew out to shoot some footage at St. Pat's.

Duncan made copies of the newspaper stories and sent them along with a letter of introduction and a sample Pilanimal to trade journals and key members of the medical community. This spawned a number of other stories in newsletters and journals as well as queries for purchasing information.

Chapter Twenty-one

Quick on Your Feet With a Helping Hand

Tom, Bob, and Richard flew from Indianapolis to Spokane, Washington one Sunday afternoon for a meeting with an important account the following Monday morning. When they arrived at Spokane International Airport and dutifully stood by the baggage carousel, they discovered what every business traveler fears—their luggage had not arrived with them. The airline promised to deliver the bags to their hotel as soon as they came in, but by midnight there were still no bags. Tom had brought a business suit in his carry-on, but Bob and Richard had traveled "casual" and were in no way prepared to dress for a business meeting. The first thing the next morning they called Nordstrom, Spokane's premiere downtown department store. The receptionist put a men's department representative on the line who said, "We don't open for another hour and a half but, if you'll come to the main door in fifteen minutes, we'll take care of you." When Bob and Richard arrived at Nordstrom, there were two sales associates and a tailor ready to greet them and get to work assembling the appropriate clothing, from suits, shirts, and ties

171

right down to belts, socks, and shoes. Before the store even opened, Bob and Richard were looking like a million bucks and ready for their meeting.

This is a true story told to me by Von, one of the Nordstrom sales associates who helped Bob and Richard. Von has also helped me with my clothing needs and always knows what I like, what sizes I wear, and—of equal importance—he knows my name. The Bob and Richard story is no anomaly at Nordstrom. Over the years, the Nordstrom name has become synonymous with superior customer service. Nearly everyone I know has a Nordstrom customer service story to tell, some example of how Nordstrom has exceeded expectations in meeting customer needs.

My business partner, Cindy, tells the story of her husband, Frank, going into Nordstrom to look at shoes. He was wearing a pair of shoes he'd purchased at Nordstrom four years earlier. He had worn them a lot, and they were beginning to look as if they'd seen better days. When the sales associate approached and asked what he could do to help, Frank joked, "Well, I bought these shoes here at Nordstrom, and they're just not holding up."

"If you're not satisfied with the shoes, we'll replace them for you," the sales person said.

"No, I'm joking, " said Frank. "I've been wearing these for years."

"Maybe so, but if you're displeased in any way, we'll take care of it."

Of course, Frank made it clear he was *completely* satisfied with the shoes. They had held up over several years of heavy use, and it was just time to buy a new pair. One thing was for sure, Frank knew when he bought his new pair of Nordstrom shoes that he could take seriously their customer satisfaction guarantee.

Good customer service consists of treating your customers the way you would want to be treated if you were in their shoes. Sounds simple, doesn't it? The concept is simple, but the execution involves the following.

Customer Focus

Your entire organization needs to be very clear about the importance of customer service, what it is, how it will be expressed in your day-to-day transactions, and what your organizational policies are with respect to handling problems. Customer focus involves building and maintaining customer relationships. This means collecting enough information from your customers to know their needs so that you can better serve them. It means looking for opportunities to enhance your relationship with your customers, one customer at a time. It also means setting appropriate expectations for your customers. A lot of your customers' expectations will follow from the positioning, or niching, that your business has done, assuming that your niche or market position has been clearly communicated. Consider McDonald's, for example. When you can't get a burger cooked extra-rare with horseradish and fresh red onions at McDonald's, you don't necessarily consider that poor customer service. McDonald's promises fast food of very consistent quality delivered quickly and cheerfully. Everybody knows that. As a consequence, you just wouldn't go to McDonald's for a custom-built specialty burger. You'd go there for standard McDonald's fare and be happy as long as you got it quickly and cheerfully. Another way that customer expectations are set is through the selling effort. It is always better to under promise and over deliver than to let the customer be mistaken about the parameters of your ability to meet their needs.

Customer Communications

An important aspect of customer service is enabling easy communications access to your customers. Be sure that your business phone number is printed clearly on all ads, coupons, business cards, notes, and letters. If the customer is seeking assistance, wishes to offer a comment, or has a complaint, he should be made to feel that your business appreciates his making contact. Follow up with customers to thank them for their business or their comments. This is a good opportunity to build the relationship and seek feedback for improvement. Always communicate customer feedback to all employees. They need the "atta-boys" as well as the challenge to continually improve their service to customers.

Customer Service Training

In addition to the need for your employees to be knowledge-able about your product or service, they may need training in listening skills and in the art of soliciting comments from customers. After all, the best information you'll ever get *about* your customers is *from* your customers. If your employees know how to use conversation ice-breakers, how to draw customers out, and how to ask questions in a non-threatening manner, they will get more, and presumably better, customer information. This has the added benefit of demonstrating to customers that your business is sincerely interested in meeting their needs and hearing their points of view.

Anticipate that there will be customer service problems. An old proverb says, "Even monkeys fall from trees." Monkeys may be the best tree-climbers in the world, but occasionally even they will have a mishap. Your company won't be any different. Train your people to anticipate problems and to use the slip-up and subsequent recovery as an opportunity to cement a bond with a customer. No doubt you, as a consumer, have had the experience of complaining to a business about something and been utterly won over by them as they strove to make it right for you. Flubbing up does not need to be a complete loss; you can turn it into an opportunity with the customer as well as an opportunity to improve your systems to prevent problems in the future.

The Cost of Customer Service

Although you might wish to give royal treatment to all your customers, it is only realistic to consider the cost of service and realize you need to draw a line somewhere. You probably can't, for example, offer free shipping and handling or customizing and delivery or alterations or croissants and espresso to every customer every time. I once read of a mail-order catalogue that established a tier system with their customers. They applied the 80-20 rule, determining which 20 per cent of their customers were responsible for nearly 80 per cent of their business. For those 20 per cent, they kept detailed database files on customer interest, tastes, and preferences and used that information to build a custom catalogue for each customer reflecting their predilections. Although the mail-order company would have liked to have done this for all their customers, the cost was prohibitive. Nevertheless, they were able to give this kind of individualized service to their top-tier customers. A somewhat different version of the tiering approach is the frequent-traveler programs at the major airlines. Generally, if you fly often, you are given a status that allows early boarding as well as points that allow for upgrading to a better class of service.

Customer Service Empowerment

Marla, one of my partner, Cindy's, friends did the bulk of her Christmas shopping in one store last year. She spent over $600 there in one evening. The store where Marla was shopping offered free gift-wrapping on any item costing in excess of fifty dollars. Marla enjoyed wrapping gifts and wanted to do most of the wrapping herself, but one gift needed to be shipped right away, so Marla asked the employee at the wrapping counter to wrap it for her.

"I'm sorry," the young woman responded, "This item is priced at less than fifty dollars. Our policy is to wrap gifts that cost fifty dollars or more."

"But I just spent several hundred dollars here," Marla explained.

"I'm sorry, ma'am," the dutiful young clerk insisted, "That's the policy."

What's wrong with this picture? I'm sure you can see right away that some further training was in order. The young woman at the wrapping counter had been listening carefully when the policies and procedures were explained to her, and she was not going to get in trouble by violating store policy. She apparently did not feel empowered to bend or even interpret policy. It is important to stress to your employees that they will not be reprimanded for making a judgment call on a customer-service issue. If they make the wrong call, in the customer's favor, it can be discussed later and policy can be clarified. But they need to feel free to help the customer when they can without fearing retribution. Your support of your employees' endeavors to service the customer can also be expressed in overt recognition for their efforts or reward programs.

Motivate Employees to Offer Excellent Service

The basics here are to hire people with strong, intrinsic motivation and good judgment. Then train them well and praise them regularly for their customer service efforts. Above all, treat your employees with consistent courtesy and respect. If you fail to do that for them, you cannot expect them to treat your customers with courtesy and respect. Build a positive environment where everyone is pulling together and knocking themselves out for the customer and for each other. If, through your leadership, you can achieve that, you will have an establishment that draws customers like a magnet.

K K K K

Duncan and Denise often met for early-morning coffee when they had planning to do. One morning they set a goal to develop their customer service policies. Since they would be doing business-to-business sales, the customer service requirements would be a little different from a retail outlet. Still, they wanted to be as sensitive to customer needs as they could be. A good start, they decided, would be to establish a toll-free telephone number and print it on all their stationery, business cards, and peripherals. They also decided to print it in large numerals on their shipping boxes. They sketched out a simple script for handling incoming calls and agreed to have a brief staff meeting to teach proper handling of phone calls to Ruth and Greg. That way, no matter who answered the phone, there would be consistency in the professionalism and courtesy with which customers were greeted.

After shipping their first big order, Denise received a phone call from the customer stating that one of the Pilanimals had fiberfill coming out through a seam. Apparently the fill hole had not been properly closed. Denise assured the customer that the Pilanimal would be promptly replaced and apologized for the inconvenience. On a couple of other occasions Denise had noticed fill holes not being completely closed. She caught it before shipping, but this was clearly something that required an extra step in inspection. The customer complaint had illuminated the need for this quality-control measure. At that time Duncan and Denise also agreed that whenever a customer was unhappy, they would attempt to resolve the problem to the customer's satisfaction within 48 hours. They sent two Pilanimals, free of charge, to the customer along with a note expressing their appreciation for his phone call, an apology for the inconvenience and pointing out that an extra Pilanimal had been included to compensate him for his trouble.

Establish Systems For Financial Operations

Chapter Twenty-two

Can We Get a Little Structure Around Here?

Going into business requires selecting a legal structure for your business. You will find this out quickly when you talk to the IRS to request information on tax obligations. The first question they will ask you is, "Do you have a sole proprietorship, a partnership, or a corporation?" Why would the IRS want to know? Because the tax implications for each legal structure are different. The other primary consideration is liability. Let's look at the different structures and how they differ.

The Sole Proprietorship

This is what you have if you go into business as the only owner. There is little, if any, paperwork to do. This is the least regulated form of business. You will have complete control over your business ,and all profits or losses will be yours. There are tax advantages in that there is no double taxation on a sole proprietorship—the business is not taxed as a separate entity, you are the business and you will report your income on a regular personal income tax form. The down side is that you and everything you own are open game in the event of a lawsuit against the business. This is a serious concern because business liability suits can be hard to predict, involving everything from slips and falls to burns from hot-coffee spills. We could rail on about tort reform here, but the point is, you may need to protect yourself. One way to do this within the structure of a sole proprietorship is to purchase liability insurance. Still, you and your family will be responsible for any unpaid debts the business may rack up, and there is no insurance to protect you from that.

If you choose to run a sole proprietorship, it will be important for you to have good general management skills and be reasonably competent in performing or overseeing all aspects of operations. Although you can hire people who have skills that you do not possess, you will need to have a basic understanding of their functions in order to manage and assess them properly.

Partnership

When two or more people agree to contribute resources and skills to operate a business and agree to share in the profits, losses, and management of the business, it's a partnership. For liability and tax purposes, the partnership is similar to the sole proprietorship in that there is no double taxation and each partner is personally liable for the obligations of the business. Within a partnership there can be general partners who participate in the operation of the business and share in the liability, and there can be limited partners who invest their money in the business but have nothing to say about its operation and have liability limited to their investment.

A partnership can be a great way to go when partners have complementary areas of expertise. It enhances the skill-pool from which the business can draw, it can mean better funding for the business since both or all partners will be contributing to start-up resources. It can also mitigate the all-alone-out-there feeling because you have your partners to look to for encouragement and advice.

Remember that going into business with a general partner means spending more time with them than you might want to, often under stressful circumstances. All general partners are legally bound by the action of any one partner. Trust in the integrity and judgment of your partner is therefore required. A detailed partnership agreement is strongly recommended to help out in the event of disputes, such as one partner wishing to leave the business, etc. No government agency requires a partnership agreement, but we highly recommend that you have one. Most people who have been in business partnerships will tell you that it is not unlike a marriage in that the relationship requires close contact nearly every day, differences in personality and working style can cause discordance between partners, and there is stress inherent in running a business that will impose itself upon the relationship. So choose your partners wisely and remember that it is a lot easier to be congenial while exploring business ideas over cocktails than it is while in the trenches. Suffice it to say that partnerships should not be entered into lightly.

The Corporation

Unlike the sole proprietorship or partnership, the corporation is a legally recognized entity of its own. Its existence continues even upon death of the owners, partners, or shareholders. It carries its own liability, which is not transferable to the personal assets of the owners. Limited liability is one of the major advantages of incorporating. Another advantage involves raising capital. Because a corporation is a more complex structure, more highly-regulated, and required to keep more detailed records, investors are likely to view it as less risky than unincorporated businesses. Corporations also have stock, which makes it easy to sell interest in the business to raise capital.

With respect to taxes, the corporation is taxed as a separate entity. The shareholders are also taxed on their dividends. If you are paid a salary by the corporation, that too will be taxed as personal income. It is also true that under certain circumstances there are tax advantages to incorporating. Having a good professional tax advisor will be important.

As I mentioned earlier, the corporation is more highly-regulated than other business structures. This means more paperwork, more government stuff to deal with, more forms to fill out and file both when starting up and from that day forward. This is viewed as a disadvantage by many, although investors may actually feel more secure as a result.

For small to medium corporations with fewer than 36 shareholders, a modified business structure called a Subchapter S Corporation is available. The S corporations are not double-taxed. Profits and losses are passed on to the shareholders and tax liability is dealt with at that level.

Limited Liability Company

A new form of legal structure, now available in 46 states, is the limited liability company (LLC). This structure is popular with small businesses because it allows the business owners to avoid double taxation yet be protected from personal liability for the business's debts. Be sure to ask your attorney about the advantages and disadvantages of this structure. The specifications and regulations can vary from state to state making this a better choice in some states than others. You should also be aware that, because the LLC is a new structure, it is still evolving legally. There may be pending legislation in your state that could change the regulations governing an LLC, affecting you if you were to chose this structure. You will need to know both the current law and any proposed or pending laws. Your attorney will also explain how the LLC differs from other structures with respect to transferability of ownership, continuity of the business, and issuance of stocks.

To learn more about the taxation differences from one business structure to another, contact your local office of the Internal Revenue Service and request the following free publications:

Publication #334   Tax Guide for Small Business
Publication #533   Self-Employment Tax
Publication #541   Tax Information on Partnerships
Publication #542   Tax Information on Corporations
Publication #589   Tax Information on S Corporations

For you computer buffs who browse the web, you'll find the IRS has a number of web pages from which you can download IRS forms and publications, including those listed above.

According to government records, the sole proprietorship is the most prevalent form of business, accounting for about 70% of all American businesses. Partnerships account for about 10%, and corporations 19%. Here's an eye-opening fact, though: of all business revenues generated in the United States, 90% is generated by corporations. The corporate structure is more conducive to growth. If your vision is to turn your small business into a large one, incorporating may be for you.

Because the business structure you choose has direct and serious tax and liability implications, it is worth the investment to seek professional advice from an accountant or attorney. Once they have studied the specifics of your business, they can advise you as to what structure would be most conducive to your success.

K K K K

At first, Duncan and Denise thought a partnership would be the most appropriate legal structure for their business. But after discussing the advantages of corporations, they agreed that a Subchapter S Corporation would make more sense. The tax benefits and protection against liability made this type of corporation hard to beat for their needs. Denise contacted an attorney, who helped them file the appropriate paperwork, and soon thereafter their business officially became Pilanimals, Inc.

Chapter Twenty-three

No Taste for Accounting?

You've balanced a checkbook, right? Every time you make a deposit or withdrawal and every time you write a check, you record the transaction. You fill in the date and include a remark identifying the transaction: "paycheck," "rent," "cash machine," etc. You put the amount of the transaction in the proper column—deposit or withdrawal—and you adjust the balance appropriately. At the end of the month, when you receive your statement, you reconcile it to your checkbook, making sure that neither you nor the bank has made any errors.

That's accounting. It's a simpler version than you'll need for your business, but it's accounting. More accurately, the daily record-keeping functions are bookkeeping, and the monthly, quarterly, and yearly reporting and analyzing functions are accounting. If you can balance your checkbook, you can understand the basic principles of bookkeeping and accounting.

In fact, if you can balance your checkbook, you already understand the most basic principles. A checking account is an *asset* account; in it you record money or value that is yours. Other asset accounts include savings, inventory, accounts receivable (money that is owed to you), equipment, and buildings.

When you take money out of your checking account, you record it as a withdrawal. An accountant would call it a *credit*. When you put money into your checking account, you record it as a deposit. An accountant would say a *debit*.

Another kind of an account, a *liability* account, is used to record money or value that you owe. Liability accounts include accounts payable (money you owe to suppliers) and notes payable (money you owe to banks). Suppose you borrow $20,000 from a bank. The balance of your notes payable account would be $20,000. If you make a loan payment of $1,000, you would debit the account that amount, bringing the balance to $19,000.

That's right. When you debit an asset account, the account increases, but when you debit a liability account, the account decreases. At first this may seem counter-intuitive, but when you consider that an increase in an asset and a decrease in a liability have the same effect on your equity, it makes a lot more sense.

There are two other account categories besides assets and liabilities that you'll work with regularly: *revenues* and *expenses*. Revenue accounts include retail sales, wholesale sales, and interest earned. Expense accounts include salaries and wages, rent, insurance, and advertising. Then there's a retained income account, but you won't have to worry about that until you close your books at the end of the year.

Whenever you do anything that involves money, whether you spend it, receive it, or just move it around, you need to account for it. You do this by debiting and crediting the appropriate accounts. Debits and credits always come in pairs. When you debit one account, you must credit another. When you pay the bank $1,000 on a loan, you have to debit the notes payable account. You also must credit your checking account the same amount. If you process raw materials into a finished product, you must credit the account that contains the raw materials and debit the account that contains the finished product.

If this is making sense to you, you either already have some training or experience with bookkeeping, or else you're just a natural. If you're completely confused, don't worry. Unless you already know what you're doing, you'll want to have an expert set up your accounting system. And whether you're experienced or not, you'll want your bookkeeping system on a computer. Your expert will help you determine what accounts your business will need, and the computer program should take care of the debits and credits. Your main bookkeeping task will be to enter the information the computer prompts you for.

A good computer program will also help you produce balance sheets and income statements. There will likely be certain reports you'll out-source to an accountant, though, particularly quarterly and yearly tax reports.

There may be a computer system designed specifically for your kind of business. If there is, chances are it will include accounting software, as well as order processing, inventory control, and other programs appropriate to your business. Otherwise, Quickbooks and Peachtree both offer good business software at affordable prices. The sales staff at your local computer or software store or the person who helps you set up your system will be able to help you select the one that is right for you. To find an expert to help you with the set up, ask around. Check with other businesses for recommendations or look in the yellow pages; you'll find several companies that specialize in helping small businesses set up their accounting.

Some business owners who dread bookkeeping and accounting when they start their companies come to find it one of the most rewarding aspects of business. After all, what could be better than counting all the money you're making? Other business owners never fall in love with it but do it because they recognize its value. Whichever category you end up in, a proper system of bookkeeping and accounting is necessary to produce the financial statements and ratios you need to manage efficiently the finances of your company. We'll talk about those in the next chapter.

K K K K

For the first year of their business, Denise had been taking care of all the accounting, so she had developed a pretty good understanding of it. As they expanded, though, she didn't want to be tied to it. So she and Duncan agreed to hire a bookkeeper to take care of the daily functions and to contract with a service for the quarterly reports.

They also needed a better system than the ledger cards she'd been using. Denise contacted three different accounting services who advertised in the yellow pages that they helped new businesses get set up. Two of them offered to send a customer representative out to demonstrate computer systems and present their services. Dell's Accounting & Bookkeeping offered a software system that seemed as though it would be easy enough to use and that appeared to suit Pilanimals, Inc., but Dell's was the only company that would be able to offer support for it. Accurate Accounting Service encouraged Denise to use Quickbooks but gave her several options that they would support. Denise liked Quickbooks and felt comfortable with the salesperson from Accurate. So Duncan and Denise signed a one-year contract with Accurate that included hardware and software setup, definition of all ledger accounts, training classes for their bookkeeper, telephone and site service and support, and processing of all appropriate quarterly reports.

Chapter Twenty-four

Balancing Act: Using Financial Reports

"They're raising my rent, Berry, and I don't know if my business can afford it." Leo owned a take-out seafood restaurant near the marina in Seattle where I used to moor the Krypton.

"How's the restaurant doing?" I asked him.

"Okay, I guess," he said. "I make enough to pay the bills and take a little home each month."

We talked a little more, and I asked him for specifics. "I don't know," he said. "I have a service do all my accounting."

"Do they send you regular financial reports?" I asked.

"They send me something," he said, "but I'm not sure what it is."

Leo's business was doing fine, but that was more a result of his clam chowder than financial management. Together we went over his recent financial reports, discovered some areas Leo needed to attend to, and determined that he could indeed afford the rent increase. (I ended up coaching him to negotiate a lower increase than his landlord had proposed, but that's another chapter).

Leo is typical of many small-business owners. They work hard and do what they do well but neglect many financial aspects of their businesses. They think that analyzing financial reports is beyond them, that it's better left to accountants and bankers, that without an intricate understanding of accounting principles no one could possibly decipher balance sheets and income statements. They're wrong. You don't need to understand the accounting process in order to read financial reports any more than you need to understand internal combustion engines to drive a car. You may not know a debit from a credit, but you can still evaluate the information presented in these reports and use it to make decisions and better manage your business. Let me show you how.

There are two reports you should know how to read: the balance sheet and the income statement, also known as the profit and loss statement. The balance sheet tells you how much equity you have in your business at a specified *point* in time. The income statement tells you how much money you made (or lost) over a specified *period* of time.

Before I explain these reports, though, let's define some terms:

Assets. Anything of value that is owned by the business. This is not limited to tangible items (see Miscellaneous Assets). There are two types of assets: current and fixed.

Current Assets. Assets that will be converted to cash or used by the business within a year. Current assets include cash, accounts receivable, and inventory.

Accounts Receivable. Money that is owed to you, usually for goods and services that you have sold on credit.

Fixed Assets. Assets that will last more than a year. Fixed assets include capital assets, long-term investments, and miscellaneous assets.

Capital Assets. Assets such as land, buildings, and equipment.

Miscellaneous Assets. Fixed assets that do not fit into the categories of capital assets or long-term investments. These are often intangible assets such as patents or copyrights.

Liabilities. Any claims that are held against the business. In other words, anything that the business owes. There are two types of liabilities: current and long-term.

Current Liabilities. Liabilities that will be paid within a year. Current liabilities include accounts payable, accrued liabilities, and taxes.

Accounts Payable. Short term debts that you owe, usually for goods or services purchased on credit.

Accrued Liabilities. Expenses for which you have already used the benefit. Commissions that have not yet been paid on sales that have already been made is an example of an accrued liability.

Long-term Liabilities. Liabilities that will not be paid within a year. Notes payable and bonds payable are long-term liabilities.

Equity. The owner's value in the business. Equity can be calculated by subtracting liabilities from assets.

Gross Income. The dollar amount of goods and services sold during the specified period of time.

Cost of Goods. The dollar amount spent to obtain the goods and services sold. This includes purchase, shipping, processing, and labor costs that are directly attributable to the goods or services.

Gross Profit. The difference between the gross income and the cost of goods. In other words, if you subtract your cost of goods sold from your gross income, you will come up with your gross profit.

Expenses. All expenses incurred to run the business. There are two basic types of expenses: selling expenses and general and administrative (G&A) expenses.

Selling Expenses. All expenses incurred in the marketing and sale of goods and services. This includes expenses for commissions, advertising, and public relations.

G&A Expenses. All expenses that aren't attributable to cost of goods or selling expenses. G&A expenses include clerical, rent, utilities, and insurance.

Net Income. The difference between the gross profit and expenses. If your gross profit is greater than your expenses, the difference between the two is your net profit. If your gross profit is less than your expenses, the difference is your net loss.

First I'll explain what goes into the balance sheet and the income statement. Then I'll teach you how to analyze each and what information you can learn that will be useful to you in managing the finances of your company.

As I said earlier, a balance sheet tells you how much equity you have in your company at a specified point in time. It does this by summarizing your assets and liabilities. See the sample balance sheet I have created for ABC Company on page 195. Assets are reported at the top of a balance sheet and are separated into categories of current assets and fixed assets. Liabilities are listed next and are separated into categories of current liabilities and long-term liabilities. Sometimes assets and liabilities are separated into narrower categories than I have shown. Capital assets, for instance, might be broken down into land, buildings, and equipment. The equity of the business is calculated by subtracting the total liabilities from the total assets. Finally, the sum of the total liabilities and the equity is listed.

So what's this tell you? It's easy to see how much value you have in the business (equity) and how much value your business is currently using (total liability and equity). But there's a lot

ABC Company
Balance Sheet
December 31

ASSETS
  CURRENT ASSETS
      Cash   28,466.12
      Accounts Receivable   23,192.59
      Inventory   15,583.07
      Total Current Assets   67,241.78

  FIXED ASSETS
      Capital   69,632.83
      Investment   0.00
      Total Fixed Assets   69,632.83

  TOTAL ASSETS   136,874.61

LIABILITIES
  CURRENT LIABILITIES
      Accounts Payable   21,215.37
      Accrued Liabilities   2,254.21
      Taxes   2,204.76
      Total Current Liabilities   25,674.34

  LONG-TERM LIABILITIES
      Bonds Payable   0.00
      Notes Payable   34,261.93
      Total Long-term Liabilities 34,261.93

  TOTAL LIABILITIES   59,936.27

EQUITY   76,938.34

TOTAL LIABILITIES & EQUITY   136,874.61

more this report can tell you. I'll show you a couple of the more useful things you can learn from it, but first let me explain the income statement.

An income statement reports your net profit for a specified period of time. See the sample income statement I developed for ABC company on page 197. Gross profit is calculated first by subtracting the cost of goods sold from the gross income. Don't confuse the cost of goods sold with the amount that you spent on inventory during the specified period. Much of what you sell during a particular period will probably have been purchased earlier, and much of what you purchase during the specified period will probably remain in inventory at the end of the period. Below the gross profit, the income statement calculates the total expenses for the period. These expenses are then subtracted from the gross profit, leaving the net income.

As was the case with the balance sheet, items on the income statement might be separated into narrower categories. Gross income, for instance, might be broken down into categories of retail sales, wholesale sales, and sales of services. Also like the balance sheet, it's easy to read and understand the basic information this report offers—in this case, gross profit, net profit, and expenses—but there are other valuable ways to analyze it as well. Let's see what else we can learn from both the balance sheet and the income statement.

Liquidity and profitability are two aspects of your business that can be evaluated by analyzing these two reports. Liquidity refers to the amount of liquid assets (assets that can be quickly converted to cash) a business has available to meet its current liabilities. Profitability refers to the ability of a business to generate a profit and show an acceptable return on investment. I'm going to show you five ways to analyze your balance sheets and income statements, each of which will help you to evaluate your business's liquidity or profitability.

ABC Company
Income Statement
December

		Totals
Gross Income	30,692.36	
Cost of Goods Sold	18,594.22	
GROSS PROFIT		12,098.14
Payroll	6,200.00	
Rent	815.00	
Utilities	386.34	
Office Supplies	77.32	
Insurance	566.67	
Advertising	845.90	
Professional Services	128.56	
Travel	0.00	
Maintenance & Repair	396.84	
Packaging/Shipping	0.00	
Miscellaneous	142.19	
TOTAL EXPENSES		9,558.82
NET INCOME		2,539.32
Depreciation	53.32	
Interest	229.55	
NET PROFIT (before taxes)		2,256.45

K Current Ratio
K Quick Ratio
K Average Collection Period
K Net Profit on Sales
K Return on Investment

Financial ratio analysis is used to identify strengths and weaknesses in businesses. This enables owners to take appropriate action to maintain those areas where their businesses are successful and to attend to those areas that need improvement. There are dozens of different ratios used by financial analysts, but two of the most common and most useful are the current ratio and the quick ratio. Both use information found on the balance sheet, and both evaluate a business's liquidity.

The *current ratio* is simply the ratio of current assets to current liabilities. Suppose we use the figures from the balance sheet for ABC Company. Current assets were $66,241.78, and current liabilities were $25,674.34. The calculations would look like this:

$$67,241.78 \div 25,674.34 = 2.6$$

ABC Company's current ratio is 2.6 to 1 (2.6:1). A current ratio of 2:1 or higher is generally considered acceptable, so ABC Company's liquidity is strong, at least according to the current ratio.

The *quick ratio* is the ratio of cash and accounts receivable to current liabilities. Let's use the figures from ABC Company again. Cash was 28,466.12, accounts receivable were 23,192.59, and current liabilities were 25,674.34. The calculations look like this:

$$(28,466.12 + 23,192.59) \div 25,674.34 = 2$$

ABC Company's quick ratio is 2:1. A quick ratio of 1:1 or higher is generally acceptable, so again ABC Company's liquidity is shown to be strong.

Although these ratios give a good indication of a business's liquidity, there are variables these ratios don't account for that may affect a company's ability to meet its obligations. One of these variables is the amount of time it takes to collect accounts receivable. If it takes too long, the money from accounts receivable won't be available when the company must pay its bills. *Average collection period* is a standard measure of this. It is calculated by dividing accounts receivable by average sales per day. Average sales per day is figured by dividing gross income by the number of days in the period. We learn from ABC Company's income statement that they had a gross income of $30,692.36 for December, and there are 31 days in the period.

$$30,692.36 \div 31 = 990.08$$

ABC Company's average sales per day were $990.08. Their accounts receivable, which we learned from their balance sheet, were $23,192.59.

$$23,192.59 \div 990.08 = 23.4$$

The average collection period for ABC Company is 23.4 days. What is acceptable varies greatly based on factors such as what kind of business you're in, what your profit margin is, and what interest you charge, if any. For an average business that offers thirty-day credit accounts, though, anything under 30 days would generally be considered good.

Net profit on sales is an indicator of profitability. It tells you what portion is left over from every dollar you receive after you pay all your expenses. Net profit on sales is calculated by dividing

net profit by gross income. ABC Company's net profit for
December was $2,256.45, and its gross income was $30,692.36,
both of which we learn from their income statement.

$$2,256.45 \div 30,692.36 = .074$$

ABC Company's net profit on sales for December was 7.4%.
Again, the acceptable rate varies tremendously. Many supermarkets are able to work on about 2% because of the volume they
sell. A jeweler, on the other hand, would need a much greater net
profit on sales. Robert Morris Associates publishes the *Annual
Statements Studies*. The data provided in this report include
standard ratios and are organized by industry.

  Return on investment is the most common and perhaps the
most important indicator of profitability. It tells you how much
your business earned for every dollar you had invested during the
specified period. Return on investment is calculated by dividing
net profit by total assets. ABC Company's net profit was
$2,256.45, and its total assets were $105,874.61.

$$2,255.45 \div 136,874.61 = .0165$$

ABC Company's return on investment for December was
1.65%. Keep in mind that this is the return for one month. This
represents an annual return of 19.8%. Anything over 15% is
generally considered a healthy business, although some businesses have returns on investment that are much greater. If a
business can't generate a 15% return, you'd be better off
liquidating those assets and investing the money in something
with a lot less risk and nearly as great a return. Or, better yet,
there may be steps you can take to make the business more
profitable.

If analysis of financial reports indicates that your business's profitability is inadequate, you can address this weakness by either increasing your gross income or decreasing your expenses. If analysis reveals insufficient liquidity, the solution is either to increase your current assets or decrease you current liabilities. Your strategies for accomplishing these goals will differ depending on the kind of business you are in as well as your specific situation, but further analysis of your financial records may suggest areas in which you can begin. For instance, if your current ratio is acceptable but your quick ratio is not, you may have too much inventory. By selling down your inventory, you will increase your cash while decreasing your accounts payable, both of which will help to rectify the situation.

There are many possible causes of weaknesses in liquidity or profitability, and most of them have a cure. The first step toward curing any financial problems that might exist in your business, though, is to diagnose them, and one useful tool in this diagnosis is proper analysis of your balance sheets and income statements.

K   K   K   K

Let's look a couple of years into the future at a balance sheet for Pilanimals, Inc. (page 202). It looks like they've built some equity into their business. Let's calculate their current ratio:

$$87,184.74 \div 33,044.22 = 2.6$$

Their current ratio is 2.6:1. How about their quick ratio:

$$(37,426.29 + 32,927.90) \div 33,044.22 = 2.1$$

Their quick ratio is 2.1:1. Both of these ratios indicate that the liquidity of Pilanimals, Inc. is strong.

Pilanimals, Inc.
Balance Sheet
December 31

ASSETS
CURRENT ASSETS
Cash	37,426.29	
Accounts Receivable	32,927.90	
Inventory	16,830.55	
Total Current Assets		87,184.74

FIXED ASSETS
Capital	22,931.18	
Investment	0.0	
Total Fixed Assets		22,931.18

TOTAL ASSETS	110,115.92

LIABILITIES
CURRENT LIABILITIES
Accounts Payable	16,152.77	
Accrued Liabilities	15,542.83	
Taxes	1,348.62	
Total Current Liabilities		33,044.22

LONG-TERM LIABILITIES
Bonds Payable	0.00	
Notes Payable	9,120.41	
Total Long-term Liabilities		9,120.41

TOTAL LIABILITIES	42,164.63

EQUITY	67,951.29

TOTAL LIABILITIES & EQUITY	110,115.92

Chapter Twenty-five

Making Projections

Projections are a necessary part of both starting and managing a business. Without projections, you have no way to know how profitable your business might be or even if it can be profitable at all. Without projections you have nothing to use as a basis for business decisions; you have no way to justify new expenses and no way to judge what new products or services might make sense for your business. Without projections you can't evaluate facility needs, equipment needs, inventory needs, and human resource needs. Projections are important to managing nearly every aspect of your business. Make projections stretching at least three years into the future, and update your projections regularly.

There are three sets of projections I encourage small-business owners to make. The first two become a resource you will use when making many decisions for your business. These two sets of projections also go into your business plan and will be scrutinized by your banker and potential investors. The third set is for your own benefit and will help to motivate you during some of the rough times, particularly when first starting a business. These are the three sets of projections:

K Sales and Expense Projections
K Cash Flow Projections
K "What if" Projections

Sales and Expense Projections

Sales and expense projections are similar to the income statement we discussed in the last chapter, but instead of reporting actual sales and expenses for a past period of time, sales and expense projections estimate sales and expenses for future periods of time. See the sample sales and expense projections sheet I developed for XYZ Company on pages 206 and 207.

To develop your own sales and expense projections, start by listing all of your expected expenses. Add these together to determine your total expenses for each month. Next list your projected sales and deduct your estimated cost of goods. This will give you your projected total revenue for each month. Then subtract your total revenue from total expenses to find your profit or loss for each month.

Make conservative sales projections that you can not just achieve, but that you have a reasonable chance of exceeding. There are few things more satisfying than beating your goals. There are also a couple of other reasons it's important to be conservative in your projections. First, it's important for you to determine whether your business can be profitable even with modest sales. You don't want to find out later that you can't afford to stay in business after a few months of not realizing lofty goals. Second, bankers and investors are more likely to be interested in your business if you can demonstrate that you can be profitable with sales they know you have a good chance of making.

Cash Flow Projections

One of the challenges of starting and maintaining a business is that you need funds available each month to pay for expenses and to cover the cost of goods, but the funds from each month's sales aren't usually available until the following month. As a result, the owner of a new business must either secure a loan or make a capital investment in order to have the funds to meet these obligations. Cash flow projections are used to determine whether your business will continue to have sufficient funds available to meet its obligations.

Notice that the sample cash flow projections sheet for XYZ Company on pages 208 and 209 is quite similar to their sales and expenses projections sheet. In fact, the top sections, the expenses, are identical, while the revenue sections differ slightly. Because funds from sales generated in one month are often not available until the following month, you'll find that the amount of sales listed for January on the sales and expenses projections sheet has been moved to the February column of the cash flow projections sheet. Likewise, funds from February's sales show up in March on the cash flow projections sheet, and every other month's sales are moved one month later as well.

As the name suggests, cash flow projections track the projected flow of cash to and from the business. Notice that XYZ Company begins with a capital investment of $50,000. After meeting all their projected obligations for January, they would have $13,870 left. After calculating February's projected receivables and payables, they would have $9,615. With these projections you can easily see whether XYZ Company will be sufficiently funded, based on their projections, to remain in business throughout their first year. If XYZ Company's cash flow drops

XYZ Company
Sales and Expense Projections

	Jan	Feb	Mar	Apr	May
EXPENSES					
Rent	2,500	2,500	2,500	2,500	2,500
Telephone	200	200	250	250	250
Furniture Lease	230	230	230	230	230
Equipment Lease					
Copier	150	150	150	150	150
Computer	250	250	250	250	250
Office Supplies	125	125	125	150	150
Insurance	150	150	150	150	150
Postage/Shipping	75	75	75	100	100
Professional Fees	500	75	200	75	75
Printing	500	0	250	0	0
Advertising	750	1,000	1,000	1,000	1,000
Salaries					
Owner	3,500	3,500	3,500	3,500	3,500
Sales Clerk (FT)	1,800	1,800	1,800	1,800	1,800
Sales Clerk (PT)	900	900	900	900	900
Cashier	1,000	1,000	1,000	1,000	1,000
Tot. Salary Overhead	1,800	1,800	1,800	1,800	1,800
Travel & Ent.	250	250	500	250	250
Vehicle Expense	250	250	250	250	250
Miscellaneous	200	200	200	200	200
Total Expenses	15,130	14,455	15,130	14,555	14,555
REVENUE					
Sales	30,000	33,000	35,000	37,000	38,500
Less Cost of Goods	21,000	19,800	21,000	22,200	23,100
Total Revenue	9,000	13,200	14,000	14,800	15,400
Profit or Loss	-6,130	-1,255	-1,130	245	845

XYZ Company
Sales and Expense Projections

Jun	Jul	Aug	Sep	Oct	Nov	Dec
2,500	2,500	2,500	2,500	2,500	2,500	2,500
300	300	300	350	350	350	350
230	230	230	450	450	450	450
150	150	150	150	150	150	150
250	250	250	250	250	250	250
150	200	200	200	200	200	200
150	150	150	150	150	150	150
100	150	150	150	150	200	200
75	75	75	75	75	75	75
250	0	0	400	0	0	400
1,000	1,500	1,500	1,500	2,000	2,000	2,000
3,500	3,500	3,500	3,500	3,500	3,500	3,500
1,800	1,800	1,800	1,800	1,800	1,800	1,800
900	900	900	900	900	900	900
1,000	1,000	1,000	1,000	1,000	1,000	1,000
1,800	1,800	1,800	1,800	1,800	1,800	1,800
500	250	250	500	250	250	500
250	250	250	250	250	250	250
200	200	200	200	200	200	200
15,105	15,205	15,205	16,125	15,975	16,025	16,675
40,000	42,500	45,000	47,500	50,000	52,500	55,000
24,000	25,500	27,000	28,500	30,000	31,500	33,000
16,000	17,000	18,000	19,000	20,000	21,000	22,000
895	1,795	2,795	2,875	4,025	4,975	5,325

XYZ Company
Cash Flow Projections

	Jan	Feb	Mar	Apr	May
EXPENSES					
Rent	2,500	2,500	2,500	2,500	2,500
Telephone	200	200	250	250	250
Furniture Lease	230	230	230	230	230
Equipment Lease					
Copier	150	150	150	150	150
Computer	250	250	250	250	250
Office Supplies	125	125	125	150	150
Insurance	150	150	150	150	150
Postage/Shipping	75	75	75	100	100
Professional Fees	500	75	200	75	75
Printing	500	0	250	0	0
Advertising	750	1,000	1,000	1,000	1,000
Salaries					
Owner	3,500	3,500	3,500	3,500	3,500
Sales Clerk (FT)	1,800	1,800	1,800	1,800	1,800
Sales Clerk (PT)	900	900	900	900	900
Cashier	1,000	1,000	1,000	1,000	1,000
Tot. Salary Overhead	1,800	1,800	1,800	1,800	1,800
Travel & Ent.	250	250	500	250	250
Vehicle Expense	250	250	250	250	250
Miscellaneous	200	200	200	200	200
Total Expenses	15,130	14,455	15,130	14,555	14,555
REVENUE					
Sales	0	30,000	33,000	35,000	37,000
Less Cost of Goods	21,000	19,800	21,000	22,200	23,100
Total Revenue	-21,000	10,200	12,000	12,800	13,900
Profit or Loss	-36,130	-4,255	-3,130	-1,755	-655
Capital Investment	50,000				
Cash Flow	13,870	9,615	6,485	4,730	4,075

XYZ Company
Cash Flow Projections

Jun	Jul	Aug	Sep	Oct	Nov	Dec
2,500	2,500	2,500	2,500	2,500	2,500	2,500
300	300	300	350	350	350	350
230	230	230	450	450	450	450
150	150	150	150	150	150	150
250	250	250	250	250	250	250
150	200	200	200	200	200	200
150	150	150	150	150	150	150
100	150	150	150	150	200	200
75	75	75	75	75	75	75
250	0	0	400	0	0	400
1,000	1,500	1,500	1,500	2,000	2,000	2,000
3,500	3,500	3,500	3,500	3,500	3,500	3,500
1,800	1,800	1,800	1,800	1,800	1,800	1,800
900	900	900	900	900	900	900
1,000	1,000	1,000	1,000	1,000	1,000	1,000
1,800	1,800	1,800	1,800	1,800	1,800	1,800
500	250	250	500	250	250	500
250	250	250	250	250	250	250
200	200	200	200	200	200	200
15,105	15,205	15,205	16,125	15,975	16,025	16,675
38,500	40,000	42,500	45,000	47,500	50,000	52,500
24,000	25,500	27,000	28,500	30,000	31,500	33,000
14,500	14,500	15,500	16,500	17,500	18,500	19,500
-605	-705	295	375	1,525	2,475	2,825
3,470	2,765	3,060	3,435	4,960	7,435	10,260

below zero, they're going to have bills to pay but no money to pay them. Then they're going to have to make another capital investment or secure a loan.

Neither sales and expense projections nor cash flow projections should be a one-time exercise. They shouldn't be something you do when you're putting together your business plan or trying to borrow money and then never consider again. They can be useful tools in the regular financial management of your business. It's important to evaluate your past projections and regularly make new ones. And the longer you operate your business, the better equipped you'll be to make more accurate, and thus more useful, projections.

Projections Versus Actual Sales and Expenses

It's a good idea to chart your actual sales and expenses against those that you projected. This can be important for two reasons. First, if you have overestimated your sales or underestimated your expenses, you need to realize it as soon as possible so you can take whatever steps are necessary to ensure that your business remains viable. Second, observing the differences in your projections and actual sales and expenses will help you in making new projections. You can chart your projections against your actual sales and expenses on a form similar to the expenses and sales projections sheet we looked at earlier. The only difference will be that you'll want two columns for each month, one for projected figures and one for actual figures. See the example for XYZ Company on page 211.

"What If" Projections

Of the three sets of projections that I suggest you make, I find the final set the most fun. "What if" projections are exactly what they sound like. Ask yourself, "What if?" What if I land a

XYZ Company
Projections Versus Actual Sales and Expenses

	Jan Projected	Jan Actual	Feb Projected	Feb Actual	Mar Projected
EXPENSES					
Rent	2,500	2,500	2,500		2,500
Telephone	200	190	200		250
Furniture Lease	230	230	230		230
Equipment Lease					
Copier	150	150	150		150
Computer	250	250	250		250
Office Supplies	125	97	125		125
Insurance	150	163	150		150
Postage/Shipping	75	128	75		75
Professional Fees	500	789	75		200
Printing	500	430	0		250
Advertising	750	900	1,000		1,000
Salaries					
Owner	3,500	3,500	3,500		3,500
Sales Clerk (FT)	1,800	1,800	1,800		1,800
Sales Clerk (PT)	900	0	900		900
Cashier	1,000	600	1,000		1,000
Tot. Salary Overhead	1,800	1,475	1,800		1,800
Travel & Ent.	250	600	250		500
Vehicle Expense	250	250	250		250
Miscellaneous	200	189	200		200
Total Expenses	15,130	14,241	14,455		15,130
REVENUE					
Sales	30,000	27,900	33,000		35,000
Less Cost of Goods	21,000	21,000	19,800		21,000
Total Revenue	9,000	6,900	13,200		14,000
Profit or Loss	-6,310	-7,341	-1,255		-1,130

particularly lucrative account? And if I prove myself with that one, what if I land three more just like it? What if a product I introduce really catches on? What if a really big company wants to buy my idea? What if I can make more money not selling it to them? What if?

I've made a lot of "what if" projections over my career as an entrepreneur. Many became reality during my time running Sylvan Learning Centers. Others came true when I sold Sylvan and became a multi-millionaire. And there are still others that I continue to work toward today.

Conservative sales and expense projections and cash flow projections are important to the financial management of your business. They are useful when making practical decisions about everyday operations. And realizing or exceeding these projections is one of the most satisfying experiences of owning a business. But if realizing and exceeding these projections is satisfying, then just making "what if" projections is one of the most exciting and motivating things a business owner can do.

K   K   K   K

Although Denise was quite busy with Pilanimal production, she always seemed to find time to work on projections. During the first several months, she found her projections were not very accurate. She tended to underestimate both sales and expenses, and while they did better overall than she'd projected, she came to view it as a challenge be able to closely predict the financial activities of Pilanimals, Inc.

As time went by, the practice of making projections and then comparing them to actual sales and expenses along with all that Denise was learning about business every day helped Denise to develop an ability to make amazingly accurate projections.

Chapter Twenty-six

Building a Plan and Planning to Win: The Business Plan

Your company's business plan is like a résumé. A résumé presents a job seeker's qualifications, his education, experience, and skills, to those who might be able to assist him in achieving his goals. A business plan will do the same thing for your company. It will detail those things about your company, its purpose, projections, and strategies, that will be of interest to bankers, investors, and employees. A business plan is a tool to use to secure the help you'll need to realize your objectives. And preparing a business plan and referring back to it can help you develop and maintain a clear focus for your business.

There are certain elements that can be found in virtually every good résumé, but beyond the basics, there are many perfectly acceptable ways to design and format a résumé. The same is true for business plans. There will be certain information that bankers and investors will look for, and this information must be clear and accessible. However, like résumés, there are many acceptable ways to structure this information in a business plan.

Now that you're nearing the end of *Return From Krypton*, you have the ability to produce the information that will go into your business plan. You're able to develop your mission statement, to generate the needed marketing data, and to work through the appropriate financial information. Once you have all the necessary information, all you need to do is assemble it into a business plan.

As I said, there are many acceptable ways to structure a business plan. You'll find many books and software packages that can help you format the information you learned to develop while reading *Return From Krypton*. Each one will take a slightly different approach, and each will tout its version as the formula for successfully securing loans and venture capital. Also, the Small Business Administration puts out business plan pamphlets specifically for small retail businesses, small manufacturing businesses, small service businesses, and others. Any of these resources will serve you well in formatting your business plan. The particulars of a business plan's structure are not important as long as those who are reading the plan have no trouble finding and understanding the information they are interested in.

This doesn't mean that the presentation of your business plan is altogether unimportant. It's important in the same way that wearing a business suit is important in certain careers. Like most business suits, your business plan's presentation should be conservative. Put your business plan in a blue, black, or brown cover, and keep the paper and type simple. Your business will afford you plenty of opportunities to express your creativity, but this isn't one of them. A clean, well-presented business plan will make a good impression and incline the reader toward your business, but, in the same way that it is the person in the suit that is important, it is the information in the business plan and the business it represents that's going make the difference.

The basic questions that a business plan should answer for a banker or investor are, "How much profit do you expect from this business?" and "What makes you think you can achieve that?" Here are the primary elements that should be in a business plan to answer those questions:

- **K Statement of Purpose.** The statement of purpose is an introduction to the business plan in which you introduce your business to the reader, explain what you are trying to accomplish with your business, and reveal what you want from the reader.
- **K Description of Business.** This will be a more detailed explanation of your business beginning with a description of the industry and including elements ranging from the legal structure of your business to descriptions of the products and services you intend to market.
- **K Marketing Strategies.** In this section, you will include much of the information you developed by using the principles discussed in the marketing chapters earlier in this book. You'll define your market and include explanations of strategies for positioning, pricing, distribution, and promotion.
- **K Competitive Analysis.** The competitive analysis explains how your marketing strategies will relate to your competitors and how large a market share you expect to achieve in your industry. You will learn this information when you do the research explained in the marketing chapters.
- **K Financial Components.** This section includes the financial projections you learned to make in the last chapter. If you are already operating your business, you'll also include the financial reports.

You should have no trouble finding a book or a computer program that will take you step by step through the process of formatting your business plan. If you have a solid idea and plan for your business, include these elements, and answer the two questions, "How much profit do you expect from this business?" and "What makes you think you can achieve that?" you'll be on your way to securing the help you need to make your business a success.

𝕶 𝕶 𝕶 𝕶

Duncan and Denise determined that they would need a loan to buy equipment and to use as operating capital during their first several months of operation. A business plan, they knew, would increase their chances of securing a loan. So Denise checked out a book on business plans from the local library and got started. Although it wasn't exactly an easy task, she found that the book walked her through it step by step. She also found that she had already developed most of the content for the business plan as she and Duncan had worked through certain principles, the same principles we've covered in this book, particularly in the chapters dealing with finances or marketing.

Once she had completed the business plan, she and Duncan scheduled an appointment with a banker they had met when they opened a checking account. The following week they were approved for a loan.

Over the next several years, Pilanimals, Inc. grew and prospered. They developed new lines of Pilanimals as well as many other products. Ten years later they were supplying hospitals and clinics all over the United States and Canada with health-care products designed to comfort anxious patients. How did they do it? Duncan had an idea. Denise helped him develop a plan. And together they put it into action.

Avoiding Common Pitfalls

Chapter Twenty-seven

Checking with the Experts

Every business owner needs professional help.

Now, wipe that smile off your face! That's not what I meant. By professional help, I mean the kind you can get from an attorney, an accountant, an insurance agent, a banker, or a well-qualified consultant.

In fact, you will need a *team* of professionals, including all of the above. From the time you make some of those initial decisions, like selecting a legal structure you need to have a competent attorney and accountant to assist you in assessing your business needs. You don't need to look far to find horror stories of people who failed to seek professional advice and came to regret it. What's more, many business-owners have run into nightmares as a result of marginal competency on the part of their attorneys or accountants. What you need are professionals who are not just competent, but *really* good at what they do. Do not skimp on effort when searching for the right people. And, if you are tempted to go the do-it-yourself route on legal and tax issues in order to save money, forget it! You don't want to stumble through that mine field alone! With competent professional help you can get your business set up right to begin with and make appropriate changes along the way to accommodate business growth.

As you begin the search for your team of professional advisors, talk to other business owners for recommendations. Interview several candidates before making a choice. In most cases you will not be charged for an initial consultation.

Attorney

Almost every business needs a lawyer who will diligently protect the business from unforeseen legal pitfalls. In selecting a legal structure, liability is one of the major considerations. Your attorney can advise you as to the structure to select and will help you set it up, filing all necessary information with proper agencies to establish your structure. An attorney who routinely advises businesses will also know what other government requirements may pertain to your business such as licenses, zoning ordinances, and any other legal documentation necessary to build the proper legal foundation for your business.

If you elect to structure your business as a partnership or limited partnership, your lawyer can help you to develop a partnership agreement. If you incorporate, there will be documents required to be filed with the state and corporate bylaws to be written. Your attorney can also help you set up a corporate record book, get stock certificates, and obtain a corporate seal.

Other issues that may come up requiring legal advice include patents, trademarks, copyrights, contracts, employee terminations, the filing of state and federal reports pertaining to your business, and a host of other common occurrences with potential legal implications.

A good lawyer who understands your business can be sure that you are in compliance with the law from the beginning and can serve to protect your business from legal problems along the way.

Accountant

Your accountant will, of course, offer services in accounting and tax preparation. It is advisable to consult with your accountant when you are selecting a legal structure for your business because there are different tax implications with each structure.

There are a number of government filing requirements that your accountant can help you with. For example, you will need a tax identification number and there will be filing requirements with the IRS, the state employment service, and possibly other state agencies. If your business is incorporated, there will be significant filing requirements with the state in which you are incorporated. Your CPA (Certified Public Accountant) can help you with all of these needs.

Insurance Agent

There are a number of ways to manage business risks. Many of them involve insurance. A good agent can help you determine what level of coverage and what combination of coverages will best protect your business without undue expenditure. It is generally best to use the same agent for all of your coverages because discounts will often apply if you carry multiple policies through the same company. You will want to talk to your agent about: liability insurance, fidelity bonds, business interruption coverage, bad-debt insurance, business owner's insurance, property insurance, and life, health, and disability insurance.

Banker

You will want to build a good relationship with a banker long before you approach that banker for a loan. Part of the reason for this is the banker's role as an advisor or consultant to her clients. Once you have established that relationship by opening an account and discussing your business with your banker, your success becomes important to the bank's success. Most bankers offer a number of supportive services for business owners including assistance with financial planning, guidance in developing a business plan, loans, lines of credit, electronic funds transfer, and credit card services.

Consultants

From time to time you may find it helpful to utilize the services of a consultant. It can be tough to know when it makes sense to pay money for someone to come in from the outside to tell you what's what.

Corporate downsizing and subsequent outsourcing during the 90s have resulted in a robust consulting market with highly-trained and experienced consultants available to assist with virtually any business challenge. From setting up human resource management systems to designing marketing plans to training in conflict management, there are specialists available to help.

When should you consider hiring a consultant?

1. When a highly technical task is required that is beyond the scope of your organization's ability. If, for example, you decided to change computer systems, you might need an information management system specialist to help you design your new setup and to train you and your staff in its use.
2. When you hit a wall. By this, I mean those times when you've tried Plan A, Plan B, and a host of contingency plans and you are still not getting the results you need. Say, for example, your marketing and sales efforts have not yielded the sales expected. You might want to enlist the help of a consultant who specializes in the market you're attempting to penetrate.

3. When you feel that thinking within your organization has become entrenched and you need someone to take a fresh look at what you're doing.

4. When you identify training needs in your staff that could be handled better or more cost-effectively by a specialist from outside your organization. Selling skills, customer service orientation, and teamwork are a few examples of training needs that can often be met efficiently by a consultant.

5. When efficiency and productivity can be increased by having a consultant set up a system for you that can then be maintained by you or your staff. During your start-up phase, for example, you may find you need a record-keeping system. You may find it cost-effective to have a specialist do the initial setup.

Some guidelines when using a consultant:

1. Be clear about what you want the consultant to do. State your objectives in specific and measurable terms. Agree on a start date, a completion date, and methods for evaluating performance.

2. Remember that you are the ultimate expert about your own business. Respect the expertise of your consultant, but do not dismiss your own critical judgment of what he or she has to say.

3. Keep your employees informed about how the business will benefit from the work of the consultant.

4. Be sure that you and your staff learn from your consultant, thereby bringing some of his expertise in-house to serve you in an ongoing way.

5. When negotiating a contract with the consultant, be sure to designate what expenses will be covered and how fees will be paid (hourly, daily, flat fee by project, etc.).

To find a consultant:

1. Ask for recommendations from other business owners, or from your banker, attorney, or accountant.
2. Seek out people who have been successful in accomplishing what you are trying to do and ask if they are interested in consulting.
3. Check trade publications, trade associations, or the yellow pages.
4. For free or low-cost consulting contact:
   a) The Small Business Administration (800) 827-5722
   b) Service Corps of Retired Executives (202) 205-6762
   c) Association of Small Business Development Centers (402) 595-2387

Expertise and *integrity* are essential attributes of a good consultant. Carefully checking references will be an important part of assessing your consulting candidate for these characteristics. In addition to experience and knowledge, a good consultant will have good interpersonal and communications skills. Be sure that the consultant will be available to fit your company's needs. Flexibility is a plus in the event that you need more or less of the consultant's time than you originally anticipate.

You will almost always learn something of value from a consultant. You probably won't end up implementing all of his recommendations, but you will be challenged by his conclusions that differ from yours, reassured by areas of agreement, and stimulated by his more objective view of your operations.

Chapter Twenty-eight

Time Keeps on Slipping into the Future

The story is often told of the man who invented the telephone. What was his name? No, not Alexander Graham Bell, the other guy. The one who had the same idea at about the same time but arrived at the US patent office two hours later than Bell. Elisha Gray registered a claim at the US Patent Office two hours after Alexander Graham Bell. Gray disputed the claim in court unsuccessfully. He went on to earn a considerable fortune from his other inventions, but was never to achieve the acclaim that Bell did with his telephone patent. This guy was as smart as Bell, as enterprising, and as deserving of success. But he was two hours too late. This is a good story to keep in mind when you need a sense of urgency.

I cannot begin to tell you how critical it has been to my success to move quickly on what needed to be done. In previous chapters I have talked about the idea of "compressing time," how you really *can* do 40 years worth of work in 10 years and retire if you set your mind to it. Since we each have a finite number of years to do all that we want to do on this planet, it makes sense

225

to quit dawdling and get on with it. The flip side of that has to do with all the Alexander Graham Bells in the world that just might beat you to your well-deserved success and usurp it. Timing may not be everything, but it plays a remarkable role in determining who makes it and who becomes an also-ran.

When I started my third major business, I did not initially plan to franchise it. But when it became clear that franchising was in the best interest of our customers and the company, I contacted my team of accountants and lawyers and got all the required paperwork done in ten days. This process normally takes about six months. But I knew I had a great idea and that action was critical. I had no way of knowing who else might be developing a similar business or what opportunities we might miss if we took six months to file our franchise papers. And, frankly, I have no interest in looking back on it. I'm committed to moving ahead *now*! If there were one critical success factor that I could give to you as a grand-opening gift for your business, it would be this sense of urgency and love of action.

Everyone is given 24 hours every day. It's what we each choose to do with that time that makes the difference between success and failure. In this chapter I will share with you a couple of techniques that have helped me to get more done in the course of a day, help my staff to stay on track to meet multiple deadlines, and anticipate needs ahead of time to keep major projects from being derailed by unpleasant surprises.

I have tried a large number of time management systems. I found that any of them worked fairly well if I disciplined myself to use them consistently and follow through with what I had planned. Over the years, I have changed calendar systems, used electronic organizers, and used elaborate project planners. I'm probably not through experimenting. Sometimes a new system can be motivating and bring a fresh perspective and renewed commitment to time management. One tool that I have never outgrown, though, is what I have come to call the Krypton project planner.

The project planner starts with a piece of 13-column accounting paper. Across the top you list increments of time—days, weeks, months, hours—whatever is appropriate to your planning needs. Down the left-hand column you list the tasks, sub-tasks, and action steps required to get the project done. You determine when that step must be completed in order to have the whole project done on time and you mark that in the appropriate time column. In this way, the project as a whole is seen as dependent upon the successful completion of the interim steps, which can then be delegated to staff members who will know why the deadlines are essential and will understand where their step fits into completion of the whole.

Another advantage to laying out the project visually like this is that you can sometimes see ways to speed up the process and move the project forward. Perhaps some of the steps could be contracted out while your staff works on other steps. Maybe there are alternatives to the steps identified, steps that could be less costly or quicker to implement. These possibilities tend to come to mind more easily with a graphic representation of the project and its timeline in front of you.

Make no mistake, learning to do things quickly will be one of the keys to your success. Tom Peters, in an interview with *The Economist* in 1989 introduced the idea of time as the new competitive battlefield. Since then, TQM (Total Quality Management) has been replaced as a buzzword in many circles by QRM (Quick Response Manufacturing). It doesn't take an MBA to know that when quality, cost, and customer-service are equal, the guy who can deliver sooner will win the day! So, once you've done your project planning based on how long you think it will take, ask yourself, "How might we be able to complete this sooner?"

There's no question that we all have many opportunities during the course of a day to make better use of our time. Certainly, one of the best ways to maximize efficiency is to stay organized. Searching through piles of paper on your desk for needed information is something you should never have to do. Your time is too valuable, and you deserve better. Establish a straightforward filing system and use it.

Prioritize your long and short-term goals. Check them against your vision and your mission to determine what is of greatest importance. Each evening, make a list of the most important things you look forward to accomplishing the following day. It plants the expectation of success in your mind and allows you the freedom to consciously leave it behind for a good night's rest.

Use your automobile cassette-player. Many excellent training tapes and wonderful books are available on cassette tape. When you consider how much time you spend in your car, this is significant time that could be used to your advantage. I sometimes listen to books on tape while traveling by air, or while doing mundane, no-brainer tasks like washing the car. I love the feeling of getting two things done at once.

If you feel a little slow in the morning, rush yourself through a few tasks. Getting some accomplishments under your belt will make you feel in control and make the rest of your to-do list less daunting.

Revisit your vision. Some people spend an hour a day doing this. They savor the details and the sensation of success. This helps them to stay focused and motivated as they proceed toward fulfillment of their vision.

Although there are plenty of tools to help you schedule your time, plan your projects, and avoid time-wasters, none of this will do you a bit of good if you don't follow through and do what you have planned to do. The element that only you can bring to the mix is motivation. Emotion is what will move you to achieve what you set out to do. The word emotion contains within it the word "motion." Remember to use your motivational drawer, your vision, whatever else really sparks emotion and passion within you.

Chapter Twenty-nine

Trouble in Paradise? Working with a Partner

There are two kinds of people in the world when it comes to money: 1) those who enjoy the process of making money and view it as "winning," and 2) those whose primary desire is to be free from the need to make money. Both people value money, but their orientations lead to different behaviors and very different motivations.

After 16 years of marriage, Bob and Janet have decided to go into business together. Bob is an etched- and stained-glass artist who specializes in large windows or interior walls as well as smaller inserts and free-standing pieces. He has done this as a hobby for many years, often donating his work to churches or community libraries. Janet has been in a corporate sales and marketing position for 20 years but is burned out on the corporate world and wants to have a business of her own. What Janet wants to do is manage the business side of operations to sell Bob's work.

Janet likes to win. Every time she manages a transaction that yields a profit, she feels a little thrill. The fun is in the winning.

Bob finds money to be a necessary evil. He doesn't like dealing with it, hates having to worry about it, just wants to be left alone to do his glass work, an activity that feeds his soul.

I met Bob and Janet at a glass expo in Las Vegas. Their different orientations regarding money and business were evident in the casino. Given what I have told you about these two, who do you think would most enjoy casino gaming?

When I found Janet, she was at the blackjack table. She seemed to be playing in order to be a good sport, but she was subdued, betting conservatively, and didn't appear to be having much fun. Bob, on the other hand, was betting freely and seemed particularly drawn to the progressive slot machines.

In Janet's opinion, all enterprises with the capacity to increase or decrease financial holdings need to be evaluated in the same way. She looked at the odds on gambling and considered the degree to which her effort and skill could up the odds: she didn't like what she saw. When she made a small bet and won, she was pleased. A $100 jackpot would make her very happy and would also make her want to quit while she was ahead.

Bob didn't seem to get too excited about a $100 jackpot and, in fact, was not very interested in playing any game unless there was a chance, however slim, of winning enough money to change his life. No matter how many $100 jackpots Bob won, he would continue playing until his money was gone in order to buy as many chances as possible to win the big one and be done with it.

Bob and Janet don't understand each other in the casino, but they don't think that's any big deal. After all, they'll only be in Vegas for a couple of days, then it's back to real life. Unfortunately, Bob and Janet are going into business together, putting their financial well-being and their marriage on the line without recognizing that the difference in the way they view money could do them in.

If Janet had a million dollars, she would use it to get involved in more money-making ventures. If Bob had a million dollars he would view that as his ticket out of the money-making-venture-world. He would view it as freedom, not opportunity.

Their different feelings about money have caused problems in the past. On one particular holiday that they both now recall with some embarrassment, Bob purchased an expensive antique jeweled pendant for Janet. It cost considerably more than Bob had planned to spend or could really afford, but it was a one-of-a-kind piece, Bob reasoned, and he wanted Janet to have something really special. When Janet received the gift, she was quiet for a time and then got openly angry. Bob was dismayed. Who wouldn't be delighted to receive such a lovely gift? he thought. Janet, that's who. She had just invested their hard-earned savings in some securities and was trying to build up their savings account again so that they could have the house painted in the spring. Earlier that year they had made the final payment that cleared their credit card debt, a high-interest debt that Janet detested. No more charging anything, she had resolved. And we'll save up for anything we might need. Janet knew that the purchase of this pendant must have set their savings back significantly, or maybe Bob even charged it on a credit card. Either way, who was he to decide without consulting her how a significant amount of their money would be spent, even if it was on a gift for her? How could he know if she would even like such a thing? Maybe having the house painted was something she wanted far more! Bob thought Janet was being insensitive and ungrateful. After all, it was his money, too, and he should be able to spend some, especially on a gift for her. Janet thought Bob was full of it—here we go again, the poor, sensitive husband, unappreciated by his shrew of a money-mongering wife! Well, you get the picture. Bob and Janet were both unhappy and said things to each other that they regret to this day.

The problem here is that Bob hates the dominance that money has over his life. Buying that pendant for Janet was an opportunity for him to spend lavishly on Janet and feel, at least for a limited time, like someone who didn't have to worry about money and could buy his wife anything he wanted to. That wonderful feeling of freedom was worth a lot of making up for it later. Janet, on the other hand, never felt that money dominated her life in any negative way. It was true she had to work hard to get it, but the process of financial planning, investing, and working toward financial goals was satisfying to her. Money's only money, but a dollar is a dollar, and each one counts.

Bob and Janet's plan to go into business together is not necessarily doomed. After all, they've made their marriage, which is a kind of financial partnership, work for all these years. In spite of their differences, they are still together. In their marriage, Janet's rational and conservative way of dealing with money provides a feeling of security for Bob and excuses him from assuming that role, one in which he would find no pleasure. For Janet, Bob's impulsiveness, his romantic bent, his artist's view of the world, add a little magic to her otherwise pedestrian existence. Janet is sure she couldn't stay married to an accountant or a stock broker for ten minutes. Bob and Janet need the balance that they provide to one another.

What could Bob and Janet do to safeguard their marriage and their business partnership? To their credit, they had already identified some issues that could raise problems for them. Bob had been doing his glass art for years and taking great pride in it, although he never made much money from it. When Janet first suggested she'd like to manage the business side of things and allow Bob to quit his day job, spend all his time on his glass work, and not even worry about marketing it, Bob was ecstatic. He trusted Janet's business instincts and had always admired her savvy. Soon, however, Janet was asking a lot of questions about the cost of materials, if less-expensive materials could be substituted, if minimum-wage employees could be hired to do portions of the glass work to increase production, if the glass could be ordered pre-cut, if certain popular pieces could be redesigned to cut production costs. Bob was uncomfortable with a lot of that right off the bat! This was *art*, after all. He didn't want to turn into a kitsch factory! Bob and Janet had talked about a lot of these issues and Bob realized he would have to give a little to make the business profitable. Janet, on the other hand, would have to allow Bob to protect the artistic integrity of the process as long as they could do so profitably. This was a big step in the right direction. Bob and Janet seemed willing to value each other's expertise and allow for some give and take to help them reach the best decisions.

Another thing that would help this couple is to do some thoughtful and honest vision work. Each partner should develop a five, ten, and twenty-year personal vision. Then, together, they should develop a vision for the business. These three visions will need to be compatible. Once the visions have been established and it is clear they are compatible, the goal-setting process can begin. Bob will find this process helpful because what he wants most is to have some security and financial freedom. Using the vision projections, Bob and Janet can determine what kind of lifestyle they will need in order to be happy and what it will cost to support that lifestyle. Thereafter, when Bob needs to curb his desire to spend, he can focus on the vision and realize that he and Janet are moving toward financial freedom as a result of his restraint. Janet will understand more clearly Bob's orientation and will be more likely to budget small indulgences along the way that will give Bob a taste of freedom, a reminder of what they're working toward.

Bob and Janet should revisit their business vision and business goals frequently. They should work toward consolidating their respective values whenever they can, rather than compromising. For example, Janet has suggested that the works Bob is most proud of should be made in limited editions. These pieces should each be numbered and should be sold with an insert containing information about the artist, the process by which the piece was made, and a card personally signed by Bob. This process will increase the value of these pieces to collectors and allow Janet to price them somewhat higher. In this way, Bob does not compromise his artistic standards, but Janet is able to achieve a good profit margin.

Although having a business partner will inevitably lead to occasional conflicts, even if you're not married to your partner, those conflicts can be productive and raise questions about the business that need to be raised. What you need in common with your partner is a vision, a set of goals, and a sense of common decency. Beyond that, it may be better that you and your partner are different, that you bring complementary strengths to the business. Open communication and respect are the critical building blocks of any important relationship and doubly so in a business partnership. Remember that you will be spending long, hard hours with your business partner. Do not enter into that commitment lightly; it won't be easy.

In the chapter on business structures we talked about a partnership agreement. It is good to have a written agreement that spells out a lot of the terms of the partnership and also spells out what will happen if the partnership fails to work and one partner wants out. With good planning and clear understandings, a partnership can give you the best of both worlds—the freedom and excitement of having your own business as well as the camaraderie and support of a committed colleague and coworker!

Entrepreneurs, Opportunity, and Action

I have a confession to make: I have a distinct preference for entrepreneurial people. I find them exciting, likable, inspiring, courageous, intractable. They always have an aura of intrigue about them as if they had a wonderful secret. When you see entrepreneurs get together there is a sense of recognition because they all know the secret. I liken it to the bond that parents have. From the outside, being a parent looks like a lot of trouble, a lot of work, a lot of expense and sacrifice. It's only from the perspective of being a parent that one understands what makes it all worthwhile. Similarly, the life of the entrepreneur—with all the risk, the long hours, the frustrations—is inconceivable to a lot of people. Why would anybody want to do that? The entrepreneur may not be able to explain why, but he knows that it's all worth it. When he meets up with another entrepreneur, there is that recognition. They belong to the same club.

The people that I bring into my businesses are entrepreneurial. They have to be. I purposely structure my compensation programs to make them, in essence, partners with me in my

237

venture. They must understand and believe in the company vision and they must be willing to work long hours for little compensation in the beginning in exchange for generous rewards as the business grows. That's the entrepreneurial journey—the vision, the dedication, and the responsible assumption of risks and rewards.

As you may have gathered from the anecdotal passages in this book, I also believe in offering opportunity to those who value it most. I respect people who negotiate well, but I don't have much time for those who make a lot of demands up front and want some kind of guarantee. There are no guarantees in life. The sooner *that* reality is accepted, the sooner a person can get on with the business of making things happen.

Be careful to bring people into your organization who are positive and action-oriented. A few nay-sayers, blamers, and victims can poison the group dynamic and dampen the enthusiasm of everyone. Sitting on one's tush and criticizing everybody else is just too easy, and there are those who find it more satisfying to criticize others than to take action to achieve and to improve things around them. Although it's important to have people who will challenge you, beware of those who complain and doubt just for the sake of negativity.

You have read in this book and in many others about the challenge and importance of keeping a positive attitude. You may have interpreted that as touchy-feely advice on how to stay happy during the tough times. Believe me, it is much more than that. Without that positive attitude, you won't make it. It's as simple as that. Furthermore, you have a duty to keep yourself motivated and excited. Your mood will set the tone for your entire organization. Your employees and your family need to see that confidence and enthusiasm in you. If they don't, they can't possibly feel positive about the future either. Don't get me wrong. I'm not saying that this will be easy. But I have never considered it an option to get moody on my people. If I need to get off by myself for awhile, go hit some golf balls or drive my car to get my head straight, I do it. But I never rain on my own parade. I care too much for my employees and loved ones to do that. As you assume the leadership role of operating a business, think hard about your duty to model the attitude and behaviors that you hope to see in the people around you. You have the power and responsibility to make it right.

It is my sincerest wish that this book will spark some insight and motivation for you. I have endeavored to write it in such a way as to share some hard-earned wisdom, to offer some encouragement, and to honestly share with you my personal point of view. We live in times of rapid change and unprecedented opportunity. Many people are still waiting for someone to give them a break. I hope this book will move you to get out there and make some breaks for yourself.

Best wishes,

W. Berry Fowler
May 31, 1996